A Landlady's Guide

RUNNING A
B&B
A Landlady's Guide

A PRACTICAL GUIDE
FOR ANYONE PLANNING TO SET UP
AND RUN A SMALL B&B IN THEIR HOME

Christabel Milner

howtobooks

Published by How To Books Ltd
Spring Hill House, Spring Hill Road
Begbroke, Oxford OX5 1RX
Tel: (01865) 375794. Fax: (01865) 379162
info@howtobooks.co.uk
www.howtobooks.co.uk

How To Books greatly reduce the carbon footprint of their books by sourcing their typesetting and printing in the UK.

British Library Cataloguing in Publication Data
A catalogue record for this book is available from the British Library

ISBN 978 1 84528 269 1

Cover design by Baseline Arts Ltd, Oxford
Produced for How To Books by Deer Park Productions, Tavistock
Typeset by PDQ Typesetting, Newcastle-under-Lyme, Staffs.
Printed and bound in Great Britain by Cromwell Press Ltd, Trowbridge, Wiltshire

Contents

List of Illustrations

Preface

M y first experience of a bed and breakfast was just after the
Second World War.

I was eight years old when my mother, who was never tolerant of
her elderly relatives and certainly never considered the idea of
sheltering them under her own roof, booked a room for a visiting
aunt. I seem to remember there was quite a choice. Eventually an
establishment was selected that was within easy walking distance
of our house. I distinctly remember feeling a bit sad that my great
aunt was not to be allowed one of our several spare rooms. To
me, she was interestingly eccentric. To my mother, she was just
plain irritating. Her earrings were always falling off, usually into
her food, as she used glue to stick them to her ears. Everything
was stuck together then. The fact that the clip had probably
broken long before the war would not be reason enough for her
to stop wearing the earrings. Everything was mended several times
over then before anything was discarded and replaced.

My great aunt sent me an Easter egg every year, loosely wrapped
in brown paper, tied with knotted pieces of string and covered
with her spidery black-ink writing. I enjoyed picking the tiny
broken pieces out of the wrapping. Chocolate was a rare luxury.

Anyway, back to my mother and the Bed and Breakfast. No
sooner had my great aunt been settled into her room, and my
mother had walked thankfully home to prepare supper (relatives
were allowed to eat with us) than there was a telephone call from
the landlady. Muffled cries had alerted her to the fact that my
great aunt was trapped under a fallen wardrobe. She had hung
her ancient fur coat, which closely resembled a brown bear, inside

the wardrobe, and the weight of it had caused this cheap piece of furniture to topple forward, pinning her underneath.

Today this would probably have involved an ambulance, and certainly questions about health and safety. My great aunt would have been able to make a great deal of fuss about the incident. But back then, by the time my mother had rushed back round to the Bed and Breakfast, the casualty had been helped to her feet and dusted down, once the landlady's husband had grudgingly appeared from his kitchen chores to lift up the wardrobe. The wardrobe may still be there in that room for all I know. I do not remember anything more being said about the matter, in fact, I think my mother thought it was quite a joke. But you would not get away with anything like this now. Remember this story when I warn you later that you must make sure all your furniture is sturdy enough for the purpose it will be put to, and if necessary is screwed to the wall. Do not take risks with anything that involves the safety of your guests.

I opened my first Bed and Breakfast in 1981. I had returned to live in England after years abroad in Central America, Singapore and Hong Kong. I had two daughters to educate, as well as a new life and an income to make for myself. The idea of running a Bed and Breakfast seemed a very promising one. I would earn money while still remaining at home, thus avoiding the complications of going out to work every day. I would be there when the children went to school, and when they came home, as well as all through the holidays. I don't remember that I ever went away for a holiday in those four years in South Devon. I was so busy, and living in such a glorious area, it never occurred to me to leave it.

We went through the usual terrifying process of my elder daughter learning to drive and life became much easier for me once she had passed her test. She had to go to the nearest large town to take this as we had neither traffic lights nor roundabouts near us at that time. Despite the novelty of negotiating these, she passed first time, so she was able to transport herself to those remote farmyard barn discos, many of which were just a grid reference on the map, and get herself safely back home again. My younger daughter roamed the countryside on a borrowed local pony which needed exercise, and we selected an abandoned dog from a London dogs' home. To complete the picture, we adopted two homeless kittens.

Our gaunt, neglected stone farmhouse, which stood with a commanding view over a small village, was soon renovated to provide accommodation for us. One half of the house was ideal for paying guests, leaving plenty of room for privacy on our side.

Gossip soon made it known that we had recently arrived from Hong Kong. Possibly the village was disappointed that we turned out not to be interestingly oriental, but all the same we had a very happy four years there. I discovered how to be independent and to earn my own living, and found that there was a life after divorce.

My children flourished at the local school. One of the school lads used to herd his father's cows through the village on their way back to their field after the early morning milking, before he leapt on to the school bus. We never locked our car or the front door. We drank glorious creamy milk every day, delivered straight from the cowshed to our door before breakfast.

I didn't have the faintest idea of how to run a Bed and Breakfast when I started. I certainly made plenty of mistakes, but I survived and I learned. I found that I liked the turnover of different people coming to stay, and the varying interests they brought with them. If, occasionally, I did not particularly take to one or other of them, I knew they would soon be moving on out of my life, so what did it matter? Some of my first guests came back to stay several times. However, none of them became close personal friends. I touch on this subject again later in this book.

I moved from Devon to Chichester in 1985 for another year of intensive house renovation. I really enjoy bringing neglected old houses back to life. I bought a town house from the actress Doris Hare, which needed to be completely updated. The cellar of this house was transformed into a bedroom and shower for my younger daughter, my older one having already left for medical school. I added bathrooms wherever I could. For one hair-raising day, the whole of the back of the house was supported on props as we put in a steel girder to take the place of a wall. This allowed us to build a conservatory on to the rear of the house to form a dining room. I mention later how you should look at your own house to see if it can be extended in any way that would increase your Bed and Breakfast potential. If you decide to do this, always be sure to obtain the necessary building regulations approval for the work you want to carry out. These regulations are only in place to make sure you finish up with a safe construction. You should also check whether you need to apply for planning approval as well. Your local council office will advise you how to apply for these consents.

The two Devon kittens, by now both handsome cats, became lounge lizards. They never left the small walled garden, which I filled with as many climbing plants as I could. I love the tangled mass of jungle gardens, and it means there is no room for weeds to flourish. I dug out what little grass there was, laying down old bricks in its place. This meant that guests could sit outside without tramping mud back into the house. I insisted that my Bed and Breakfast guests could only smoke out in the garden, so it had to be an attractive sitting area.

My town house Bed and Breakfast soon attracted the Chichester theatre crowd, both those who were working there or those attending performances. During that period of my life I met some fascinating people. I discovered that most actors like to lie in bed late into the morning, and then they are out of the house most of the night. This makes them easy guests to have around as they are never under your feet. I was often given complimentary tickets to performances, and I even managed to rub shoulders with a few celebrities when I was invited to after-show parties. I particularly enjoyed one lovely trio of dancers who took advantage of my large wall mirrors to practise their routines.

I ended this interesting social part of my life when the opportunity came up to buy an old, derelict forge. This was attached to two equally dilapidated cottages. This forlorn collection was sitting empty and awaiting demolition, as it was considered to be beyond repair. It had been ransacked repeatedly, as there were no doors left and very little of the windows and roof. Some of the old blacksmith's tools and farm implements must have been well over a hundred years old. I wonder where they ended up? Old Frank, who had been born in one of the cottages, had died there some 79 years later. He had been unable to go up the stairs for many years before his death. These were completely rotten and dangerous. The upper floor was occupied by pigeons and bats, their droppings encrusting the floor. We later discovered that bats and squirrels occupied the roof space.

I threw away the demolition consent and set about the long, loving labour to save the building by creating from it one large cottage. The roofless smithy, which must have rung with the clang of the blacksmith's hammer for many years, became a roomy, sun-drenched kitchen. I learned the art of flint knapping as the outer walls were restored. There was a lovely overgrown garden with its own well and several heavily laden damson trees. A rusty corrugated iron privy outside was the only convenience. This was in 1987. We had to lay down mains for water, gas and electricity. Old Frank had always used the water from the well in his garden until one day he pulled up something nasty in his bucket. After that, for years until he died, he used to draw his water from the small brook that ran in front of the property. This was full of eels, and occasionally trout that had escaped from the fish farm further upstream. The first job was to build a bridge over this so that cars could get in and out. The horses would have simply waded across to be shod.

Four years later I was open for business again. The cottage became a successful Bed and Breakfast that was near enough to Chichester to still attract the theatre crowd, as well as the Goodwood set in the racing season, and the many tourists who flock to this attractive area of the country. It was a peaceful setting for a Bed and Breakfast, and guests loved studying the photos that had been taken of the extensive restoration work as it progressed. Most were impressed with the result.

Then my life changed course again, as life often does. I decided to move to Normandy. I made plans for a life in France. The

Devon cats, lounge lizards of Chichester and finally mouse hunters of the old forge, had both died by now. I like to think they both led varied and happy lives. I obtained a canine passport, by getting the necessary anti-rabies vaccination, for the spaniel who had replaced our rescued Londoner. The spaniel was also a rescued dog. I had found him cowering all alone on the side of a busy road.

But then, at the last minute, I changed my mind about France and settled instead for a small market town. I set up home again in what had been the sergeant's house attached to the former police station. There were no cells, these having long ago become my next door neighbour's kitchen. A Bed and Breakfast right in the centre of town attracts a large variety of guests. More of that later on.

The advice in this book, which all comes from my own experience of over 20 years as a Bed and Breakfast landlady, is intended to help and encourage anyone who is thinking of setting up and running a small Bed and Breakfast in their own home. I really hope that the tradition in this country of small, sometimes even eccentric, Bed and Breakfasts will be preserved. Foreign visitors love them as much as we value them. These Bed and Breakfasts, and their very individual landladies, are part of British life. It will be an irreplaceable loss if creeping bureaucracy is allowed to encroach, and turn comfortable, characterful Bed and Breakfasts into regulated anonymous boxes.

This book is intended for those of you who want to retain the tradition of the small Bed and Breakfast, by running one in your own home, and it is dedicated to those of you who are already doing so.

Part One

Finding out What's Involved in Running a Bed and Breakfast

1

Understanding the Reality of Running a Bed & Breakfast

Y ou will sometimes hear people remarking that they quite fancy the idea of running a Bed and Breakfast themselves. They think it might be something they will get round to doing one of these days, perhaps when they stop working. 'I mean, how difficult can it be?' they shrug.

'It must be dead easy. All you need to do is cook bacon and eggs. And make a few beds, I suppose.' Here they pause, and start to look thoughtful. Then they continue:

'Well, I suppose it could mean that your spare room is tied up some of the time. And I suppose you have to wash the sheets. But think of all the money you get for just doing that!'

As this conversation continues, if it does, the voices begin to sound less confident. So they should, because they are so wrong.

It most certainly is not dead easy to run a good Bed and Breakfast. It takes hard work, commitment, and attention to detail, all in equal amounts. All the time. If you think you can take up the idea of running a Bed and Breakfast as a casual, lucrative hobby, you will find that your business does not prosper, and you will not make any money.

KNOWING WHAT GUESTS WILL EXPECT
People will shop around to find out where they can get the best value for their money. They will look at several websites, make

phone calls and ask for friends' recommendations. Guests expect a high standard of comfort and cleanliness. They want good food, properly and safely prepared, and a cheerful, personal welcome from the landlady. Many want their children to be welcome. Fewer, but still a significant number, want you to welcome the family dog as well. They do not want anonymity, nor do they expect to find every place they stay in to be identical to the last. They expect to be as comfortable, or more so, than they are at home – and many people these days have *very* comfortable homes.

Long gone are the harridan landladies of the 1950s, terrorising everyone under their roof with endless house rules, and who could get away with shooing their Bed and Breakfast guests out of the house by ten in the morning, locking the door against their return until four in the afternoon, come rain or shine. And woe betide any guests who arrived late at the set mealtimes.

I should mention here that I think it is a mistake to take the attitude that Bed and Breakfast guests should be grateful to stay in your lovely home. Of course it is your home and people should behave reasonably. The vast majority of them will do so. But do not forget that they are paying you for a service. If you pay for a service you have a right to expect it. If you think you would have a problem with offering this type of service to people, some of whom will not be the sort of people you are used to dealing with, then becoming a Bed and Breakfast landlady may not be the job for you.

GETTING STARTED

The obvious thing that you must have to start your own Bed and Breakfast is one or more spare bedrooms. These may already be sitting idle and empty in the house, or you may have thought of adding on rooms. These added rooms could mean freeing up the kids' rooms, or even your own by converting the attic into an extra bedroom. I do not think converting an attic into a bedroom for paying guests is viable; it is better to keep your more conventional rooms for paying guests. You will face a lot of regulations once you go above your first floor with paying guest bedrooms. You should remember that turning your attic into a room that is considered 'habitable' (as opposed to just storage space) will require building regulations, whoever is going to sleep up there. So keep guests on the ground or first floor as it will make things easier.

Considering an attic conversion

The easiest route to a successful roof conversion is to hire a specialist who does the job all the time. He or she will discuss your requirements and whether your roof space can provide these. He or she will then submit plans to the building inspector. Your expert will then discuss any points that the Inspector may raise, will pass these on to you, and the two of them will almost certainly iron out any problems without you having too much to worry about. You will just have to pay the bill, so do your sums carefully to make sure that the bedroom you have thus freed up for letting is going to bring you in sufficient profit to make the whole thing financially worthwhile.

Also think carefully whether you, or whichever family member is moving up to the attic, will really like being up there. Most will, in my experience. Attic rooms can be most attractive and unusual. You can put in all sorts of cupboard space against the sloping ceilings, and the window will give a wonderful view of the surrounding area, with the birds flying past at eye level.

Building regulations

The building regulations regarding attic conversions change all the time, mainly about what sort of access staircase you are allowed. However, it is now generally becoming much easier to expand your house up into the roof, provided you can deal with the problem of providing sufficient strength to take the additional weight of the new floor, and whether you can get enough light and headroom up there. The fire escape problem has been mainly solved by the availability of windows designed specifically for roof rooms to allow quick and easy escape. These will be a compulsory requirement for your building regulations.

Converting your garage into a room

Garages are not always used for cars these days, and are often just a convenient area to dump things. Sort this junk out and sell what you can, take the rest to the charity shop (someone will be grateful for it) or the tip. You can then think about converting the garage into an extra bedroom, thus freeing up a family bedroom in the house for paying guests. This idea would be popular if you have teenagers. They will be able to come and go independently. Or you may want to put your paying guest into the newly converted garage bedroom. This would work if you include an en suite bathroom.

You may prefer the idea of a bedroom for paying guests that is completely separate from your home. In this case, think about a straightforward extension to your house which provides an extra bedroom and bathroom. Incorporate a door to the outside, and your guest will have independent access. This would give you an excellent custom-built letting room. Think about how the guest will get from the bedroom to the room where you serve meals. Guests do not expect to climb over messy toys in a playroom, or walk through a crowded family kitchen to get to their breakfast.

Once again, my advice to you is be sure to do all your sums before you start, to make certain that the initial outlay of expense is going to result in a reasonable income from the letting of the room, or that the extra bedroom is likely to add value to your house when you come to sell it. An estate agent would be able to advise you whether this money is well spent with regard to the future value of your house.

DECIDING WHICH ROOMS TO LET

Once you have decided which bedrooms and bathrooms are to be let out to guests, you will find it easier if these rooms are kept solely for the use of paying guests, which means that they are always absolutely ready for use. Of course you will still be able to put visiting friends in them, but you must remember that rooms let out for money must not be allowed to become a convenient dumping ground for piles of ironing, dressmaking and no longer needed dog baskets. This is not the place for that overflowing box waiting for the next jumble sale to come along.

Preparing the rooms for your guests

You must make certain that all the drawers and cupboard spaces are clean and empty. Do not make the mistake of storing some of your winter clothes in one side of the cupboard in the belief that your guest will not notice. They will, and it will let the room down badly. Likewise, never store boxes of your possessions under the guest bed. You are going to need to keep that area very well dusted.

The cat must be discouraged from ever going into guest bedrooms, however cute he may look fast asleep on the bed. Many people are allergic to cat hair, as well as many other types of animal hair. I have twice been asked if I keep dogs in my home, and I have had to say that I do. This has resulted in the guests stating politely that they will have to find somewhere else as they are allergic. In both cases I was able to recommend another Bed and Breakfast where I was pretty certain there were no pets around.

These dedicated rooms should be regularly cleaned and aired, even when they are not in use. Cobwebs grow overnight. These horrors particularly like hanging down from the ceiling corners, just out of your reach. Buy a long-handled lightweight feather duster for this purpose.

You should set up these rooms from the beginning to be let out. Do not fall into the trap of allowing yourself to regard them as anything other than ready to be used at a moment's notice, by a complete stranger. A complete stranger who is going to pay you money for their use. A moment's notice may well be all you will get if you answer the doorbell and find a suitable-looking guest standing on your doorstep. Be prepared. Have the room ready.

Preparing the bathroom

Your chosen guest bedroom should have access to a bathroom that is either attached (en suite) or is outside but not too far away. By bathroom, I mean shower or bath (or both), toilet and washbasin. Obviously the en suite option is the best, and there are an increasing number of people now who will not book a room without an en suite bathroom. But there are still lots of people who will be happy with a bathroom which is conveniently close to the bedroom.

The same rules apply to the bathroom as they do to the bedroom. The bathroom must be kept clean and ready for use at all times.

It must be free of anything that has not been put there for the comfort and use of your paying guest. A string of underwear drying over the bath, or signs that the goldfish has been given a run in the basin will not do your business any good.

Sharing a bathroom

Guests who do not know each other usually prefer not to share a bathroom. This used not to be the case. It was not that long ago when houses, even large ones, had just the one bathroom, which was used by everyone. Sometimes there was an extra toilet, often outside by the back door, but not always. Now, this is not so. Many new houses have en suite bathrooms attached to all the bedrooms, and certainly most hotels do. So this is likely to be what your guest is used to. This means that a communal bathroom for your paying guests is far from ideal. However, guests not expecting private facilities, and who are paying a lower rate, may not object to this arrangement, if the bathroom in question is a good size, and particularly if there is a separate toilet.

Bathrooms and toilets ideally should be on the same floor as the bedrooms as guests will not expect to go up and down stairs to use the bathroom.

I do feel though that a bathroom that is shared between you, your family and paying guests really is a non-starter for a Bed and Breakfast these days. So if it is really only possible to have one bathroom in the whole house, you should forget the idea of running a Bed and Breakfast in that house. I expect there will always be a few guests shopping around to save money, who may not object to the inconvenience of sharing the family bathroom. I would not like it, and I do not think your family would like it either. Your bathroom should be a private and personal place, so give this matter some thought.

Installing a macerator

You may already be aware that it is now possible to put basins, showers and toilets into all sorts of unusual places by using one of those neat little electrically run macerators. These small white boxes are usually installed behind the toilet. All the water from the shower and basin, plus what you flush down the toilet go into it. It takes all the liquid and waste, grinding it up as necessary, which allows it to be discharged out as liquid into the sewer via small bore pipes. This means you do not have unsightly waste pipes running all over the house, which are very difficult to disguise.

But these wonderful machines do come with the problem that they make quite a noise when in use, especially if used in the silent dead of night. I believe that they can now be quite well insulated, and I suppose they make no more noise than a toilet flushing, but the noise is unfamiliar, and lasts longer. The other warning note, if you are going to install a macerator, is that nothing other than what is completely natural can be put into the toilet. They do accept toilet paper! They will make an awful mess of macerating anything else, and usually give up trying. Then, they block up, and things get unpleasant. Clearing them when they stop working is a messy business, to be avoided. It is much better to put a small notice up to warn guests, and always make sure that you have provided a small bin lined with a plastic bag beside the toilet.

I used a macerator successfully for many years, installed in a tiny bathroom complete with shower, toilet and washbasin. It also dealt with the waste water from the washing machine, AND everything was pumped uphill, as the bathroom and washing machine were installed in a cellar. So do not give up on the idea of a bathroom until you have explored all the possibilities.

Here's my own solution to the bathroom problem. In one of my Bed and Breakfasts I let out my main bedroom with a separate private bathroom on the same floor. Once the main bedroom was let, it retained the private use of the bathroom for the duration of the let. This worked well, although of course it meant I could not accept any bookings for the ancillary room (I had two letting bedrooms at the time). If the guest booking the main bedroom also brought along friends or family, to occupy my ancillary bedroom, then I assumed they would all be willing to share the one bathroom. I did always mention this when accepting the booking, and the idea was never rejected. This slightly complicated system did of course put a limit on the number of guests I could take, but it was the only way I could think of around the problem. It did keep up the price I could charge for the main bedroom when it retained private use of a bathroom.

Sometimes, when I had two singles wanting to book into the two rooms, they would agree to share the bathroom, especially when I offered to drop the price slightly to allow for this. Sometimes you will have an opportunity to discuss this sort of problem with guests when several arrive on your doorstep at the same time. Making a small discount in the price will usually seal the deal to your advantage.

You should think carefully before installing an en suite bathroom in a bedroom where the noise of the macerator (which you will almost certainly have to use to get rid of the waste) will disturb a neighbour on the other side of the wall, whether this is still within your own house, or in a terrace or semi-detached property.

BEING CHILD FRIENDLY

The larger your letting bedroom is, the better. You will have the space to provide a travel cot or to put up an extra folding bed for a child. If you want to be a child-friendly business (not everyone does), you need to buy a travel cot and a high chair, ready for when the booking comes. Do not assume you can use up any old cot or high chair that you have put away in the attic. These days there are all sorts of standards for nursery equipment, so make sure your equipment, in particular the cot mattress, conforms to these standards. Buy new, from a reputable store. Mine have had plenty of use.

Don't forget that equipment like this that you have to buy for your business is tax deductible, so keep every receipt. (More on this subject in Chapter 8.)

I do not charge for children under three, so there is no profit in taking them, but you will lose some adult bookings if there is not space for the children, as well as some very delightful small guests. You may have reasons for not welcoming children, and that is your choice. You should state clearly in your brochure if you do not accept children below a certain age. If you do not welcome children, this age limit is usually twelve.

Do be aware that any pets you have in the home may not feel quite so welcoming to children as you do, so keep all pets out of the way unless you are absolutely certain of their temperament towards unfamiliar small people who may want to poke and prod them.

CATERING FOR YOUR GUESTS

Now that you have sorted out the bedrooms and bathrooms you have to consider where your guests will be eating the delicious breakfast, and perhaps their evening meal as well, that you will be preparing for them.

Very occasionally you will come across a Bed and Breakfast that only serves breakfast to guests on a tray in the bedroom. The tray is placed outside the door with a discreet knock at an arranged time. There must be a few busy people who want to be on their way, and don't eat much in the way of breakfast anyway, who would welcome this arrangement. It can be done quite elegantly, with fresh fruit and juice, and warmed rolls. But I think it is impersonal and not what people expect from a Bed and Breakfast.

Most of your guests will be looking forward to the good old traditional British breakfast served at the table. It is part of the experience, and often is something that they consider a luxury, having given up preparing breakfast for themselves at home. In the space of one generation, we have gone from breakfast being a substantial, cooked meal (nearly always fried) to a rushed grab of a piece of toast or a bowl of cereal, often eaten standing up.

Be sure to state in your brochure (more about brochures on page 35) if you intend to serve breakfast in the bedroom. It won't appeal to many guests.

Does your house have the right sort of dining room, or a large enough kitchen to feed your guests in? If you have to go to the lengths of building a conservatory or some sort of extension to create a dining room for your guests, you must first consider whether this expense will be recovered by the success of your business, or whether it is likely to significantly increase the value of your property, therefore making it justifiable. In most cases, these additions can only increase the eventual resale value of the house, but this is not always the case. So take professional advice. An estate agent would be able to give you an opinion.

Offering separate or shared tables

There is always discussion about whether it is preferable to have several small tables or to seat your guests all together around one large table. I really recommend the separate tables when you are serving breakfast at the same time to several people who do not know each other.

I will always remember having to eat breakfast closely seated (too closely) around a table with my fellow guests, who were all strangers to me and my heavily-pregnant daughter. We wanted to chat and a small table for the two of us would have suited us so much better. Of course there are gregarious, friendly people who will always enjoy getting matey around the breakfast table, but I think these are in the minority. Breakfast time is well known for being the time of day that many people do not feel like chatting, least of all to strangers. If, however, you regularly take in people who are spending the day together, say a field centre group or people coming to attend a particular course, they may well appreciate sitting all together as they will have things in common to talk about.

Set yourself up with some small square tables that can be put together, or set up separately as required. With nice tablecloths on them, these could just as well be the cheap plastic garden variety, which are so light and easy to move around. These can also be easily dismantled and stored away when you have not got a crowd to feed.

MANAGING ALONE

The next thing to consider, perhaps the most important thing if you are living alone, is whether you can manage the running of a Bed and Breakfast on your own.

If you are not living alone, it is also most important to consider whether your partner is as willing as you are to become involved with the guests. These guests after all will be complete strangers to you. Some will be very pleasant from the outset, some will mellow as they recover from their journey, or interview, or whatever has brought them to your house. A few will be odd, and even fewer probably even downright unpleasant. Some people just go through life being unpleasant, and a few of these may end up with you. Some people really dislike the idea of having to wait on strangers, or wait on anyone at all for that matter. They will view having people in their house as an unwelcome invasion of their privacy – never mind the money that it is bringing into the household. Such people will not make good Bed and Breakfast landladies, and if you happen to be living with someone who dislikes the idea of strangers in the house, and you are not certain you can keep them separate from the guests, think again about how successful your business is going to be. (Let alone the complaints you will get from your partner.)

Think really hard about whether you will feel relaxed yourself with strangers sleeping in your home. I would definitely have been happier on one or two occasions not to have been living alone in the house, but those were rare occasions. It is quite possible for women on their own, or men for that matter, to run a successful Bed and Breakfast, and many are doing so all over the country. Study my suggestions carefully about personal safety as outlined in Chapter 7 (you will develop your own strategies for these rare contingencies).

But please forget the idea of opening a Bed and Breakfast in your own home if your family are dead set against the whole idea. They are unlikely to get used to it with time, and they will make your life a misery for inflicting guests on them. A partner who is going to glare at the guests, obviously resenting their presence and their demands on your time, will be no help to you at all. Just as important, the guests themselves will feel unwelcome.

It may be sensible too, to forget the idea of a Bed and Breakfast if you are a really shy or nervous person yourself. You need to feel relaxed about the idea of welcoming guests into your home. Of course, this will become easier as you become more experienced at dealing with a variety of people. Most new landladies are bound to feel apprehensive about their first few guests, until they realise that it is really quite easy to keep people happy. But if you do think you are unlikely to get used to the idea, you will probably not enjoy running a Bed and Breakfast.

THINKING ABOUT HEALTH AND SAFETY

Before you open your front door to the public, remember there are some basic health and safety aspects to think about in your home. You may not ever have considered them before, but you are dealing with the public now, so things are very different as you have a responsibility for their safety and well-being.

Health and safety is really a matter of common sense. At the moment, if you limit your number of guests at any one time to six, you are not required to register with your local council. You will therefore escape some of the more onerous requirements of registration that affect larger businesses. A maximum of six guests is quite enough for a small Bed and Breakfast to handle, many are much smaller. I would say it is more usual for small businesses to let out one main bedroom with perhaps one ancillary bedroom, at the most two. That means at most three or four guests at a time, some of whom may be children. You will find that is plenty, if you are on your own. Especially if they bring two dogs with them, and a baby that cries all night!

Carrying out a fire assessment

A responsibility rests on every Bed and Breakfast landlady to carry out a fire-risk assessment of their property. This applies to even the smallest businesses, so do not ignore this responsibility.

It would be sensible to go over your property, imagining to yourself that it is filling with smoke and flames. Remember that smoke inhalation is one of the most likely killers in a fire. Think how your guests would exit the property. Write down your assessment briefly and keep it on file somewhere safe. It will show, if this ever becomes necessary, that you have taken a responsible attitude to the risk of fire. It means you have taken a sensible look at what might happen if there ever were a fire. Consider carefully how people would get out. Once you have thought about this, put in place any reasonable precautions where necessary. You might consider fitting fire doors to the letting bedrooms. These have to be fitted with automatic closing systems, so they are always shut, but they do give extra time to escape from the room before they break down in the event of a serious fire.

When I took a long look at escaping from my own bedroom, I realised that the little office next door has a large fixed window that I could smash in an emergency. I could then get out via a gently sloping roof, on to a flat roof next door. No one would choose to do this for fun, but fire is sudden and very frightening. Think hard about how your guests would get out of their bedrooms in the event of a fire.

Should you consider buying one of those fire escape ladders that fold up small into a cupboard? You would have to fix something secure for the ladder to be attached to. This could be a discreet hook securely fastened into the wall. No point having an escape ladder if there is nowhere to fix it to.

Be aware of the extra problems of evacuation for disabled guests. It is necessary to think all this through before you start taking in guests. You are responsible for their safety in your home.

You should get into the habit of making sure the corridors and stairways are always kept clear of any clutter. You will not be sleeping guests anywhere higher than the first floor of your house, because to do this will mean much more stringent fire precautions.

If you are considering using a room above the first floor for Bed and Breakfast guests, or if you are thinking of taking in more than the six guests allowable under the more flexible fire safety rules, then the best way to ensure that you are complying with the additional fire laws is to contact your local council for details regarding fire safety. These will all be sensible precautions, intended to save lives, so you should have no objection to carrying them out before you open for business. But they will be more stringent and therefore involve you in extra expense. You must work out whether the extra guests, or the fact that you are going above the first floor, will make this expense worthwhile. It is a lot easier to keep to the 'six guests maximum' and not above the first floor, if you want to keep your safety rules easier and more flexible.

Fire extinguishers

The fire extinguisher that you always keep in your kitchen must be regularly checked according to the manufacturer's instructions. This also applies to the fire blanket. These two should be positioned where you can grab them in a hurry, not tucked away out of reach.

Smoke alarms

Every floor of the house must have a smoke alarm fitted. These need to be checked regularly. Most of them make a bleeping noise that you will notice when the battery is running low. But they can run down unnoticed, especially if you have been away on holiday, so make a note in your bookings book or diary to check them regularly.

Be sure that you carry out this most simple of fire precautions. It is easy to overlook this job when you are busy. A smoke alarm may save lives in your house one day.

PREPARING FOR MAINTENANCE PROBLEMS

WARNING! Never be tempted to have electrical repairs carried out by someone who is not a qualified electrician. It is against the law, and you may well end up with dodgy electrics – or worse.

Before you really get going with your Bed and Breakfast, when you have got your house up and running and you are ready for your first guest, it would be sensible to rehearse the simple maintenance tasks that could crop up when you least expect them. These jobs always need attention on Saturday evenings, or when all your DIY friends are away. Bank holidays are another favourite time for disasters, and of course that is when you will be extra busy.

Make sure you know where to turn off the water, gas and electricity if you have to do this in a hurry.

Be sure that you have a suitable ladder to reach, for example, the ceiling in your bathroom. My ceilings are all very high. It is compulsory in a bathroom to use a shade over the bulb that fits flush to the ceiling. This means the bulb is not hanging on the end of a convenient length of flex, which would make the job of changing the light bulb so much easier! Get rid of flush fitting shades that have fiddly little screws to hold them in place. These will drive you mad if you have to fiddle with them. Replace them with shades that screw up quickly into place, neatly encompassing the bulb. Have a trial run by yourself, before you are faced, like I was, with an impatient guest pacing around outside on the landing in his dressing gown. My bathrooms have no windows so it is total darkness if the bulb blows. Quite alarming for the guest in a strange bathroom. Remember it would not be acceptable to leave a replaced bulb uncovered by a shade to be sorted out later.

Anticipating electrical faults

It is wise to anticipate that common electrical fault – the complete blackout. This is likely to occur ever more frequently in the future, so we are warned. The electricity in your house will fail at the most inconvenient time possible, such as when your guests are first walking through your front door. They have had a long, tiring journey, and want nothing more than to sink thankfully into the room you have ready for them, and to put the electric kettle on for a cup of tea. Make sure you have a powerful torch ready. Think about boiling a pan of water on the gas stove, to produce tea if this seems appropriate. Open up some nice biscuits.

Modern trip switches are so efficient that they will click down when a bulb blows. This, and the fact that you must use a qualified electrician, is why fewer people are being electrocuted at home. Before the trip switch goes one day, you should consider the following:

◆ Would you be able to locate a suitable chair to stand on to reach your fuse box to reset the trip switch?

◆ What if the fuse box is located under the stairs, behind the vacuum cleaner and the ironing board? Do you keep a torch (with a working battery) near to the fuse box?

◆ Do you actually know where the fuse box is?

Strangers arriving in an unfamiliar house may begin to feel alarmed unless you can get the electricity working again quickly.

If the fault does not lie within your house, and this fact will soon be obvious if your neighbours are all in darkness, then produce more torches. Candles may be romantic but these would definitely be a fire hazard in these circumstances. Keep candles for the dinner table.

Preparing for emergencies

Go over in your mind all the various emergencies, large and small, that you have had to deal with over the past few years. Ask yourself how you would cope with a bunch of strangers relying on you. Chances are, you would manage perfectly well, but think about it and be prepared.

You may well be asked to sort out a television or a DVD player that is in a guest's bedroom. You should make yourself familiar with all the sets in your letting rooms. They are probably all operated slightly differently. You may not want to linger too long in a guest's bedroom, fiddling with the television. This will come up again later in my advice for your own personal safety.

Could you remain calm if a guest became locked into their bedroom or the bathroom? A well-known actress once got herself locked into her bathroom while she was staying in my Chichester Bed and Breakfast. The cheap, fiddly lock decided to stick in the wrong place. I managed to release her using a screwdriver, and her cooperation. Luckily, she was most amused by the incident. I took out the lock and replaced it with a surface-mounted sliding bolt. I am all in favour of simplicity.

Do you understand how a door handle works, especially the older ones? You may have lovely Victorian doorknobs, so check these occasionally to make sure the little screws holding the metal spindles through the door are secure. Guests will be surprisingly rough on all your fixtures and fittings. They will slam and bang where you might handle things much more carefully. Guests expect everything to be in full working order. Remember, making excuses for broken equipment makes you sound unprofessional.

You may also have to deal with the situation of one of your guests being taken ill while staying with you. Remember this is a most distressing situation for the guest concerned. They will feel helpless and probably frightened as well, especially if they are travelling alone. You can contact your own doctor's surgery for advice, as the guest is a temporary resident in your house. Or you can phone NHS Direct for advice. If you can see that the problem is not too serious, the best plan may be to offer light meals and drinks in the guest's room, until they recover. You could offer to telephone friends or family who may choose to come and collect the guest. It is sensible to keep a well-equipped first aid box in your house for minor accidents.

SOCIALISING WITH YOUR GUESTS

'You must get to know such a lot of different people,' is often the remark made to me. 'You can't ever get lonely!'

I would never advise setting up a Bed and Breakfast with a view to improving your social life. You are much more likely to curtail it, as you will be spending a lot of time waiting for guests to arrive, or leave, or just hanging around because you are worried about leaving them alone in your house. Leaving guests alone in the house is something you will learn about from experience. I find, now after years of experience, that I can usually judge, almost from their arrival, whether the guest is one I would be happy to leave alone in my house if I had to nip out shopping or to walk the dog. I do not often go out for an evening if I have guests, as I find I am not able to relax, worrying about what might possibly have gone wrong back at my house. It never has of course, but you never know when disaster will strike, and it is better to be there when it does.

You are seldom likely to get to know your guests other than superficially, even those who end up staying with you regularly. I would not consider having anything other than a purely professional approach to my paying guests. They are using my Bed and Breakfast as a service. They are not visiting as friends. You are useful to them as somewhere convenient to stay when they need it. You need their money. So it is mutually beneficial. But it is not a likely way to make real friends. Bed and Breakfast guests, pleasant as many of them turn out to be, are just like ships that pass in the night. So I recommend keeping a detached friendly attitude. Keep your letting bedrooms free of personal photographs that might encourage your guests to comment, and learn to politely avoid questions about yourself that you feel are not appropriate, or that you are unwilling to answer. Be charming, always, but firm.

TAKING BOOKINGS

Bed and Breakfast bookings mainly come as two types. One is the spur of the moment, 'let's stop now' variety, which means the guests could arrive five minutes after they have telephoned you. That is why it is essential that your rooms are always ready. Then, there are those looking for accommodation weeks or even months ahead. These bookings are usually for holidays, weddings or parties. You must be sure that you are willing to commit to being around for these far in the future dates. You should not take the attitude that these forward bookings will be easy to cancel if or when you receive a more lucrative booking nearer the date, or an invitation to an exciting party for yourself. These people have made an effort to plan ahead and commit to you, so do your best to honour their booking.

Taking a deposit

I would, in the case of a booking in the future, ask for a deposit before I guaranteed the booking. I would probably ask for a cheque for 10 per cent of the total charge, and I would expect to receive it within a week. You must be certain to confirm the booking, the amount and the receipt of any deposit received in writing and keep a copy on file. Whether you are willing to return the deposit if the booking is cancelled would depend on the circumstances at the time. As with all small businesses, you should be prepared to be flexible. Use your own judgement. You may think the guest is carelessly messing you about, or you may be prepared to believe that a genuine reason has caused the cancellation.

Setting up an answerphone service

It is important to have an answerphone facility on your phone. It is just not businesslike to have a telephone that rings away in an empty house. The guest will not phone again. There is always another Bed and Breakfast telephone number they can try. It is preferable to use your own voice. It is so much more personal. Make sure this is a friendly, welcoming message (smile while you are recording it, your smile will come through in your voice!) stating clearly that the caller has the right number, and that you will ring back as soon as possible if they leave a number. Always call back promptly, even if the caller has mentioned a date for a booking that you cannot manage. They will remember your courtesy and possibly try you again at a later date.

Always carry your mobile phone with you. If you use a small diary for your bookings, you can have it with you all the time so you are ready to confirm dates even if you are out on the beach, or shopping in the supermarket, when the call comes. If you tell the prospective guest that you will call back once you reach home to check your bookings, you may find they have booked somewhere else by then.

Of course it is possible to cancel a booking in a genuine emergency, and no one would expect you to do otherwise, but try not to do it for any other reason.

Being available for your guests

You must accept that most guests do not want to find themselves alone in an empty house when they may need assistance, or just someone to chat with. You need to be prepared to stay around your house when you have Bed and Breakfast guests. This does not mean you cannot go out at all, but do not be away too long.

Providing a home from home

Over my long career as a Bed and Breakfast landlady I have sometimes found the need to do this. I took in a very feisty little old lady of over 80 who had been stranded in the area when her son was injured in their car. She could have stayed nearer the hospital, but I made a fuss of her, with sandwiches for her supper after a long day, and a willingness to chat about her problems. She chose to stay with me even though it meant a bus ride to visit her son every day, during his lengthy stay. Be prepared to go the extra mile with your guests and you will often be rewarded by them staying longer, or returning to stay again. Over one winter, when I am usually less booked up, I took in the temporary pharmacist from our town chemist. The chemist had had no luck in advertising for a permanent pharmacist, so they had to take one from a London agency. I explained to this very pleasant young man that this was to be a week by week arrangement. I knew there would be one or two days when he would have to make alternative arrangements, which he was quite willing to do. As I will mention later on in the book, you need to make a clear distinction between Bed and Breakfast guests, and lodgers.

I hope I have given you some idea of what it is like to be a landlady. There will often be quite a heavy demand on your time and energy, but other times it will be quiet and your guests will hardly bother you at all. There is no way of judging who will be the perfect guest, and who will seem to need an awful lot of attention. You will get a fair mixture of everything, so be ready for everything!

So now you have learned a little more about what's involved, are you sure you want to run a Bed and Breakfast?

Here are some points to consider:

- Can the guest bedrooms and bathrooms be kept in a state of instant readiness?

- Do you have a room that is suitable for serving breakfast?

- Have you considered your ability to manage on your own?

- Is your family as enthusiastic as you are about the idea of strangers in the house?

- Are you confident that you can undertake simple maintenance work when necessary?

- ◆ Will you be able to accept that guests are paying you for a service, and that they are not part of your social life?

- ◆ Can you be committed to bookings that are made weeks, even months, in advance? Are you willing to spare some time to your guests, if they need it?

2

Establishing Whether There's a Market for your Bed and Breakfast

I t is quite possible to run a Bed and Breakfast business in any area of the country as there is always a need for this service. However, some areas are undoubtedly better than others, so how busy you are going to be, and how much money you are going to earn, will depend on where you live.

People are very mobile now, so Bed and Breakfasts are needed everywhere for a widely varying number of reasons.

CONSIDERING WHO YOUR MARKET MIGHT BE

Running a Bed and Breakfast is like waiting for the bus. You will go for days without any phone calls, then suddenly within one hour you will receive three requests for bookings, all for the same date. Talk to everyone in your area about your Bed and Breakfast, once you are open for business. Let everyone know what you are doing.

You may not attract much passing trade if you are living in a lonely farmhouse, or if your home sits in an isolated country hamlet. But you should remember that these are two places where you could develop yourself a specialist market. What about attracting the people who crave solitude? They may want to watch birds or wildlife, or just wander in lonely unspoilt countryside. They may want to sit out on open moorland, painting or composing music and poetry. They all need somewhere to sleep and have a good breakfast. Hunt around for the relevant magazines that cover the sort of activities your area could offer. There is a magazine out these days covering almost every activity. Put in an advert for your Bed and Breakfast, emphasising anything you can offer that is different, like 'solitude', 'complete peace' or 'breathtaking views'.

'Are you a nudist B & B?' I was occasionally asked on the phone when I was running a Bed and Breakfast in the vicinity of a well-known nudist beach nearby. I suppose it was a logical conclusion to some people. Make certain you understand the difference between naturalists, who want to study nature and wildlife, and naturists who want to spend as much time as possible without their clothes on. If you are tempted to offer accommodation on these lines, do some research first to make sure both you and your guests understand what is on offer.

Analysing the local market
Centres for leisure activities are a growth area in this country. Centres are springing up all over the place where you can take part in all sorts of activities. If there is one of these near you make sure you have given them details of your Bed and Breakfast so that they can pass these on. Even if it is a centre with its own accommodation, this will sometimes get over booked. They will use you for the extra rooms needed, or recommend you for people looking for independent accommodation.

Keep a look out for any courses being held locally. Perhaps there is a patchwork shop that offers courses lasting several days. Those ladies would love to stay in a nearby friendly Bed and Breakfast. Art and photography, music and creative writing are all areas that are likely to offer courses lasting several days, or a long weekend. Lots of the people attending will be staying one or more nights away from home. Why not in your Bed and Breakfast? Be interested, know something about the course involved.

Even an industrial site is not without promise. One of the units in the industrial site near me makes highly specialised aircraft parts. Temporary specialist engineers frequently come there for up to several weeks' work. These engineers stay at my Bed and Breakfast because I made sure my details were available to the human resources manager. I made a point of going to see her personally when I delivered some of my brochures, so she remembered, and recommended me.

I worked in conjunction with a Field Centre in South Devon, when I had a Bed and Breakfast near Slapton Sands. The Field Centre, always very popular and busy, paid me to accommodate the number of overflow students attending in the summer, which is their really busy season. The accommodation in the Field Centre dormitories was pretty basic, so to be fair to all the students, the Field Centre insisted that those who were billeted with me had to use their own sleeping bags, and had to share rooms, just as they would at the Centre. So there was no washing of sheets for me. I received less money per person, but more people. It was fun, like running a boarding school with nobody staying for more than a week. I adjusted my evening meal to be cheap, filling and appealing to kids. Lasagna, macaroni cheese, spaghetti bolognese and any pudding with custard featured strongly. My own teenagers loved it. Be flexible and adjust to taking in guests whenever you see an opportunity.

Distributing your brochures

Distribute your details whenever you have a chance. Whenever you go out and about locally, think to yourself: should I leave some brochures here?

Do not forget the breakdown garages. These come into contact with people who have had to interrupt their journey unexpectedly. Nursing homes have visitors who sometimes need to stay nearby when they are visiting their relatives. Your local hospital notice board is another good place to advertise. They have large movements of temporary staff, as well as those people who may want to stay close to relatives in the hospital.

Forging a reciprocal arrangement with other Bed and Breakfasts
You will have competition from other Bed and Breakfasts in your area, maybe in the same road. Make it your business to find out what they are offering and how much they charge. Send them your details, and offer to recommend them when you are fully booked yourself. They will usually reciprocate the favour. Being able to recommend an alternative is always good when you have to turn down a booking from a prospective guest, and it is usually very much appreciated.

Make sure the local hotels have your details, they may well pass these on when they are fully booked themselves.

Marketing to estate agents
Estate agents are another possible source of guests for you. They will pass on your details to any customers house hunting in the area. These potential purchasers are often keen to stay a few days in the area to which they are planning to move. You will be able to answer all their questions about schools, restaurants, bus services and lots of other things they will want to hear about. Local knowledge is valuable, make sure you are full of it.

Estate agents who are on their toes will be pleased to get to know you, your property and your business, with an eye for doing business with you in the future. They know that once you are successful you may well be tempted to sell. Then, you will need their services.

Advertising in the parish magazine

The parish magazine, whether you attend the church or not, will welcome your advertising revenue. A friendly Bed and Breakfast round the corner is an excellent solution to many people who do not want relatives in their house 24 hours a day. (Remember my mother!) Perhaps their house is small, or their tolerance level will be stretched too far. With a bit of luck they will be able to arrange for you to take in the relatives, and even the relatives' annoying dog as well. You will make money (don't forget to charge for the dog) and they will be only too relieved to have some time to themselves, and to know that the dog is not sleeping on their sofa!

On page 34 is the advertisement I put into the parish magazine with just this in mind. This advertisement was provided by a generous artistic friend. I think he has caught the idea of an overcrowded house very well! I have had many bookings from local people for their friends and family as a result of this relatively small expenditure. Many of the local people come to the door to make this sort of booking. I always offer to show them my rooms, if they are vacant at the time. This reassures them that their relatives are going to be comfortable. And you will be absolutely charming, so everyone will be happy.

Too Many Guests?

**House Bursting
at
the Seams?**

Use my Bed & Breakfast

Christabel Milner [Telephone No.]

Advertising This advertisement showcased my B & B in the local community and parish magazine – that encompassed South Molton market town and several surrounding rural parishes.

The advertisement targeted local residents with the aim to supply them with an 'overflow' for friends and family visitors at times such as for holidays, weddings, funerals, etc.

It was reasonably priced and proved effective in generating a steady income stream, not subject to the vagaries of the holiday season. Once taken up, regular visitors often made repeat bookings.

PRODUCING YOUR BROCHURE

To widen your market you will need to have a brochure. I have included on pages 36 and 37 an illustration of the brochure I have liked best of all the brochures I have had designed for my Bed and Breakfast businesses. It was printed on A4 sized paper, which folds neatly into three to fit into the envelope with any letter I might also be sending.

Design and spelling

Take care with the design of your brochure. It is the introduction for your business, so it is very important. I have seen many with spelling mistakes, or which fail to give me the information I am looking for. When I received the proof for my brochure from the printer I found I had to read it several times to make sure of accuracy, and then I nearly missed one spelling error. Also, when you are abbreviating instructions (which are obvious to you because you know the area and the parking), you may not always make yourself clear. Any parking or direction instructions that are misunderstood by your guest will be blamed on you by the guest when he finds he has been given a parking ticket, or he has taken the wrong turning at the end of a tiring drive to get to you because the instruction on the brochure was ambiguous.

Always get someone else to proofread for you, this is a far more accurate method. Once the brochures have been incorrectly printed, it is an expensive mistake. A brochure with an inked in correction is unprofessional, and the subconscious impression you are giving of your business has already gone down a notch in the mind of the reader.

My brochure picture was supplied by the same artist who did the cartoon for the parish magazine. It is part of a bigger sketch

SOUTH MOLTON

A small, busy, market town dating from early Saxon times, on the southern fringes of Exmoor.

It offers individual and 'different' shops, a swimming pool, tourist office, museum and a working honey farm.

The attractive and interesting architecture is well worth a walking visit via the excellent Heritage Trail.

It has a market every Thursday and Saturday in the historic covered Pannier Market.

South Molton is an excellent base from which to explore wild Exmoor, North Devon's beautiful countryside and pretty villages.

Agriculture is still the region's main economy, some of the oldest farms have their origins before Domesday.

The spectacular surfing beaches of North Devon are within easy driving distance. (Dog lovers note that Saunton Beach is open to dogs all year round.)

There are many attractive and varied places to eat and drink – both in the town itself and in the surrounding country and coastal villages.

[NAME OF B & B]

The imposing red brick building in [name of street] was built in 1894, as a part of the town's police station.

Later, the adjoining police station itself was converted into two further residential dwellings.

Apart from the installation of modern comforts, the [name of B&B] remains almost unchanged – retaining its original late Victorian doors and windows.

HOW TO FIND US

From junction 27, on the M5, take the A361 to Barnstaple.

Take the South Molton exit.

In South Molton 'square' take the left fork into [name of street].

[Number of house] is a Victorian, 3 storey, brick building on the left-hand side, next to the jewellers.

Junction 27 to South Molton = 30 minutes.

BED & BREAKFAST

[NAME OF B&B]

[Full address]

[www.webaddresshere.com]

2007

CHRISTABEL MILNER

[Telephone No.]

[Email address]

WELCOME
to
[name of B&B]

CHILDREN

Children are welcome and we can provide a high chair and travel cot.

DOGS

Well-behaved dogs are welcome, for which there is a small extra charge. Dogs can, by arrangement, be looked after for reasonable periods whilst you are out.

ON ARRIVAL

If you are going to arrive late, or with tired children, supper or sandwiches can be ready for you.

DURING YOUR STAY

You will find many interesting pubs and restaurants in the town and the surrounding area, but simple home-cooked supper can be provided for you, if you prefer. You are welcome to bring your own wine.

FACILITIES

Double room with private bathroom on your own floor. A second double room (twin), on the same floor, is available should you require it.

You have a kettle in your room, tea, coffee and biscuits, television and DVD.

Ironing board and iron, hair dryer are supplied. A dog basket can be provided; please ask when you book.

This is a **No Smoking** house, but if you would like to smoke, or just sit outside and read, please do use the courtyard garden.

There is a large public car park behind [name of B&B]. You may also park in [name of street] for up to one hour and overnight between 6 p.m. and 8 a.m. and all day Sunday.

TARIFF
and
BOOKING ARRANGEMENTS

Bed and Breakfast

£25 per person per night

(10% reduction for 3 or more consecutive nights)

Supper

£12 per person

Children

Prices by arrangement

Dogs

£2 per dog per night

PAYMENT

By cash or by cheque, drawn on a UK bank

We are *unable* to accept credit cards

This was my most successful brochure. It was designed for me by a kind friend who has much experience of small businesses. I feel it gives all the relevant details that I was offering at that time. You could adapt the wording in my brochure to fit in with what you are offering in your Bed and Breakfast.

showing his grandson taking breakfast in the garden with his grandparents.

What you should include in your brochure

It is surprising how much information you can get into a small brochure. Your address, phone contacts and price are very important. Mention any special attractions in your area. Be clear about your policy for taking children, and what facilities you can offer for them. Be wary of offering babysitting. I have occasionally babysat for guests' children, but only after I have assessed how well behaved they are likely to be. Occasionally, guests have just assumed that they can leave the children asleep in the room while they go out. This should only happen with your express agreement, and a mobile phone number for you to phone the parents if need be.

State clearly how to find the house, and what the parking situation is, and as mentioned already, provide clear and precise directions. If you can include a map, even better.

State your policy over taking dogs. I welcome dogs and allow them to be left with me when the owners are attending a wedding or any other daytime function when the dog would get too hot if left in their car. I have never had any trouble from the many travelling dogs that have stayed in my Bed and Breakfasts. On one occasion I went out to help a guest with his luggage. It was late evening, and in the darkness of the car boot, I spied what appeared to be a young camel lying down. But this turned out to be a delightful, very large and well-behaved Gordon setter. I love dogs, and I enjoy having them to stay. But if you do not welcome the idea, state this clearly in your brochure.

Make sure you update your brochure regularly, you may need to change bits of it, particularly your charges. Do not have too many brochures printed at one time because if you need to alter something it is preferable to reprint. It will look so much better.

PRODUCING YOUR BUSINESS CARD

At the same time as you get your brochure printed, order some small business cards. These are very useful. I show here a picture of mine, which you will see is very simple. The vital information is your telephone number. These cards are slipped into wallets and you think they will be forgotten. But they may pop up later when accommodation is needed.

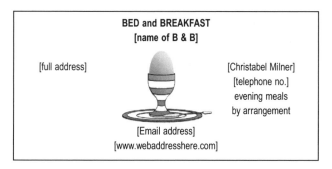

I have given out business cards to fellow dog walkers on the beach, which provided guests at a later date. I once got into conversation with a sales assistant in a London shop, giving her my card as I left with my purchases. She still stays with me regularly when she comes to Devon on holiday.

Sometimes small shops will agree to display your business card, as it does not take up too much space.

USING YOUR LOCAL TOURIST INFORMATION CENTRE

Many of my guests come via my local tourist information centre. TICs will display your details when you register with them. This registration fee is well worth the expense. They will also add your information to their website, which is useful, even if you have your own website. All coverage of your business is good. Make the effort to get to know the people working in your local TIC. Talk to them to find out about the kind of accommodation that is most needed in your area. You may be able to fill a gaping hole in the market with your business.

Many people still make the local TIC their first point of contact for accommodation, not everyone relies on the internet, even today. We landladies need to keep the TICs in business, so work with them – it will be mutually advantageous. If for some reason the guest has not paid the TIC the percentage of the booking due to them, be sure you go along as soon as possible and pay it. TICs do a valuable job for your local town. Support them.

CREATING YOUR OWN WEBSITE

Before you set about creating your own website have a look at some existing ones. Some are really awful, some are beautifully simple and clear, and make you want to phone up and book a room immediately. Most are something in between.

When I researched this subject, I found myself becoming increasingly bored, then irritated, by the screeds of stuff, including photographs, that I was expected to wade through about the owners of the Bed and Breakfast I was looking up. I was given unwanted information about their careers and their family. Don't go on an ego trip. Potential guests want information about the accommodation, the food and the surrounding locality of your Bed and Breakfast. They need facts: exact location, how to find you, price, facilities offered, etc. If you welcome children and dogs, make yourself sound welcoming. If you can provide facilities for the disabled, make that clear (for more information see page 52), and if you want people to have their evening meal with you, say something good about your cooking, and your ability to source locally produced food. Remember though, what you advertise on your website or in your brochure, you must be able to provide. Potential guests want the information fast and digestible, or they will move on to the next site, and you will have lost a sale. Do not overload your site with pictures. People are more likely to read the information than to study photographs in detail, but a photograph of the bedroom is useful, as it will tell potential guests far more than a written description will.

You do not have to be a computer expert to set up your own website. I most certainly am not gifted in that area. I sat down with a friend who has much experience with helping small businesses. She arranged for her daughter to take some excellent photos of my letting bedrooms, my walled garden showing an inviting set of table and chairs, and one of my dining room with fresh flowers on the table, hopefully looking just the place where a guest would like to sit down to breakfast.

We mulled over words and descriptions, and once the whole thing was roughed out, she arranged to send it to a web designer who finalised everything, and put it online for me. I received from him all the details and references I needed when I wanted to put up a small message that I was away and would answer booking enquiries as soon as I could. All I had to do was to remember to post up this message before I left on holiday, and to remove it when I returned. Enquiries for bookings came thick and fast on to my email. I was then able to phone and talk to the potential guests. I do prefer to talk to guests before I agree a booking. I would say the majority of these enquiries were European, but I have also had several Australian visitors via my website. On page 43 is an illustration of my own website.

Although I am a strong advocate for local TICs I do realise that the internet is here to stay. Even a small Bed and Breakfast business will benefit from its own website, although as yet I would not say this is essential for the success of your business. So if you really do not want to have any dealings with a computer, just forget the website. The local TIC will put you up on their computer without you having to lift a finger or think anything technical, and pass on potential bookings to you via the telephone. There are still plenty of people who can live without total reliance on a computer, and who choose to have human contact in all their business dealings.

Now that I have made some suggestions to you about possible markets and you have had a chance to think about this, consider the following points carefully, as you work towards your decision about starting a Bed and Breakfast.

By now you should have established whether there is a market for your B&B. Here are some points to remember:

- Be aware of what is going on in your area.
- Emphasise any special attraction about your area.
- Circulate your brochure widely.
- Always carry some business cards.
- Set up your own website.
- Make full use of your Tourist Information Centre.

BED & BREAKFAST

[full postal address]

CHRISTABEL MILNER

[Telephone No.]　　　　　**[Email address]**

Welcoming and comfortable accommodation in town centre.
Within walking distance of all amenities.
Children and well-behaved pets welcome.

- Large Double Room
- Twin Room
- Private Bathroom

Home-cooked evening meals, using local produce, available if required.

- Bed & Breakfast – £25 per person per night – for 1 or 2 nights.
- 10% discount if staying 3 or more consecutive nights.
- Children are most welcome.
- Children's tariff by arrangement, please ask.
- Cots and high chairs available.
- Pets welcome
- Strictly *NO SMOKING*.

Websites – include some photographs alongside essential facts and information

3

Ensuring Your Current Home is suitable to be a Bed and Breakfast

LOCATION, LOCATION, LOCATION

Location, location, location. Never were three truer words spoken when it comes to property. Or more specifically, your property that is to become your successful small Bed and Breakfast. Be realistic when you have in mind the type of guests you think you will attract. If you want family groups on a seaside holiday, or enthusiastic walkers, do not target this market if your house is a tedious hour and a half's drive from the beach or the moor. Those people will find somewhere to stay that is nearer to where they want to be.

Business people want to be right in town, so do people travelling by public transport. A person coming to attend an interview for a job in town would not usually want to stay on an outlying farm, even if it is surrounded by wonderful country views; but someone who is on holiday in the area might well prefer the experience and not mind the extra driving involved.

It is possible that when it comes to location, you are neither one thing nor the other. Think about this carefully. It might be better to look for a more obvious area for a successful Bed and Breakfast business. If you have really decided that this is going to be your life and your income, this might be a sensible move, especially if, like me, you do not mind moving house provided the move is going to be to your advantage. On the other hand, people come to a Bed and Breakfast for the most unexpected reasons, and you might well build up a very nice business in an apparently unpromising area. Sometimes you just have to try it for a while and see how you get on.

ADAPTING YOUR HOUSE FOR BED AND BREAKFAST

Most houses, unless they are really tiny, can be adapted to take in paying guests. But this will depend on your own circumstances. You may need a lot of privacy, or you may not mind the guests sleeping in close proximity to your own bedroom, say on the same floor. You may want to have all your family on the top floor, and just let the first floor to paying guests. Or you may live alone and want to make the maximum income, in which case you might be happy in a tiny room off the kitchen, so that all the other bedrooms are available to guests, maximising your income. You may feel that you will be so busy, you only need a room big enough to sleep in.

When you sit down and consider your house with strangers in it, you will probably feel the need to make adjustments. Perhaps a seldom used dining room could be transformed into an attractive ground floor bedroom? Some downstairs toilets can be adapted into wet rooms, which would give you an extra shower. This might not be ideal for guests, but you could use it for yourself, so it would free up the main bathroom for one of your letting rooms. You have to accept the fact that when you open a Bed and Breakfast business you will have to give up some of the peace and privacy of your home. You must consider carefully how you will feel about this. Most particularly, if you are not living alone, you must consider how your partner or your family will feel. If they hate the idea outright, then my advice here would be to give up the idea of running a Bed and Breakfast now.

Should you move house?

If you are really struggling to see how your house could be adapted to accommodate the number of guests you need to achieve a reasonable income, sometimes it is better to consider moving.

Do your sums. Consider the area you live in – is it going to bring in people looking for Bed and Breakfast? Are you absolutely sure this is the right way for you to earn an income? If the answer is 'Yes', then go out and look for the perfect house to set up your business and set about moving to start your new life. You may find a house which is already being used as a Bed and Breakfast, then half the work has been done for you. But in actual fact, there are not many houses that cannot be adapted to take in paying guests, using ingenuity and imagination, as much as cash. The whole point about small Bed and Breakfast places is that they are unusual, sometime eccentric, but above all, warm and welcoming to guests. You must get that bit right. A bleak, unwelcoming approach to the house, dreary decoration with depressing, outdated bedrooms will not bring you repeat guests, and your business will founder, no matter where you are living.

Using the conservatory

A conservatory can easily double as an attractive dining room. You will need to make sure there is sufficient heating in the winter. Remember that any room used for paying guests must be tidy and clean. Make sure you are not in the habit of dumping unused flower pots, half-dead plants or sacks of compost in the conservatory. Keep it fresh and tidy, with a lovely view over your garden. You have to make sure it is a lovely view, of course! Don't forget to cut the grass, and do a bit of weeding occasionally. When you are really busy, rely on pots of colourful annuals placed in attractive groups, just where your guests can see them best. Guests love to walk out into the garden so have a few chairs out there. I used to serve breakfast in my conservatory, or actually outside in the walled garden. I have even served supper in the garden, when the heat of a particularly hot day was retained by the high walls. Your guests can always retire into the conservatory if necessary.

Carrying out alterations to your house

You should bear in mind that structural alterations carried out inside your house must comply with any building regulations currently in force. These regulations become more stringent every year. Do not make the mistake of taking the attitude that it is your house and therefore you can do what you like, and anyway no one can see what you have done. You will need to produce evidence that you have complied with building regulations when you come to sell your property. You must pay particular attention to the safe design and construction of stairs, attic and garage conversions.

You could find yourself in trouble if a guest sues you as a result of an accident on your premises if you are not covered by the building regulations for the area where the accident occurred.

The staircase in your home may be unusual, and possibly potentially dangerous. Of course, this is perfectly acceptable, so long as it was legal at the time it was put in. That is, before building regulations really came into force for domestic buildings. But it would be sensible to take the precaution of fitting extra stair rails for safety. You are showing that although there is nothing illegal with the construction of your stairs, you are going out of your way to make sure your guest is safe. It is not your fault if the guest chooses not to hold on to the extra rail.

Creating extra rooms

I once turned a room in my garden into an extra letting room with its own bathroom. It created a perfect room for guests with a wakeful baby, or a dog, or often both of these. It also offered access for a wheelchair. I should point out that this small building had originally been constructed with a proper foundation, as I knew I would eventually put it to this use. You cannot expect to turn any old garden shed into a letting bedroom. I do know of one landlady who sleeps in her potting shed, on a camp bed up against the rake and the spade. She lets out her own bedroom in order to accommodate the maximum number of guests during the lucrative, short summer season where she lives. But this is an exceptional case, where the monetary reward is high and of a short duration. I admire her, she deserves the large sums of money she makes over these few weeks.

You have to consider the British weather. Your guest is not going to enjoy crossing the garden in pouring rain to reach breakfast in the main house. A covered walkway might be the answer, perhaps decoratively draped with climbing plants. This was not practical in the case of my garden room, so I just provided several large umbrellas, and made sure that the path was kept as puddle free and non-slippery as possible. Most of my guests loved that room, often requesting it when booking again. One lady hated it, and said she spent a sleepless night worrying about the nocturnal garden noises.

BEING AWARE OF POSSIBLE ACCIDENT BLACK SPOTS

There are usually areas in a house that are more likely than others to be the site of accidents. The staircase is one. My staircase is wide, safely carpeted and with a sturdy handrail. In spite of this fact, I have on three occasions had people fall down the stairs. After the first one, I requested all guests to put on the light when they left the bedroom at night to visit the bathroom just a few steps away. To get there, they have to cross in front of the top of the stairs. There really is no problem with this, as it is a wide corridor and all flat, carpeted flooring, with no steps. But there is a problem if you decide not to put on the light because you do not want to disturb your sleeping partner.

So, in the middle of the night last year, I was awoken by a loud bumping sound. There could be no doubt about it. The male guest that I had warned to put on the light, had not done so, and had taken a right turn at the end of the corridor, thinking he was turning into his bedroom, and instead had gone straight down the stairs.

I began to get out of bed when I heard his girlfriend come out of their bedroom and ask him:

'You all right, darlin'?'

'No, I am not!' (Only he put it stronger than that.) 'And I got no clothes on, neither!' Again, his language was stronger than I have used here.

I heard her help him back to bed, and I heard the their door shut. Then it all went quiet again. I went uneasily back to sleep.

The next morning, she informed me that he had fallen down the stairs. He then appeared himself, very embarrassed at having done just what he had laughed about the day before. He certainly had not put on any lights, and admitted that it was all his own fault. I asked him if he had a headache, or double vision.

'No, unfortunately,' came his rueful answer. 'Wish I had. I've only got one eye. It would be a bonus!'

You could not meet a nicer guest than this one. It was his second visit. I suggested his girlfriend drove him to the local hospital, just to make sure. I think I already knew her answer before it came:

'Oh, no. I can't drive!' So I took them to the casualty department of the local hospital myself. He was absolutely fine. He has been back to stay with me since, and we laugh about the incident.

I recommend you leave a small lamp with an eco-friendly low wattage bulb burning all night in any of the public areas of your home. Explain to the guests why it is there and request that they do not turn it off. Using an energy-saving bulb will cost you next to nothing.

So you see how careful you have to be with stairs. I will add that none of these three guests who fell was drunk. One of the really heavy drinkers that I have to stay occasionally also fell down the stairs – all the way down, making the most awful racket. This was less to do with the lack of light than with his inability to negotiate the steps. There was a bit of a silence after it happened, then he got himself back into his room, and everything went quiet again. In the morning he had no recollection of the event and I did not mention it. But he was very surprised at the extensive bruising he suffered, puzzling over how it had happened. He was also a very nice guy. As I say throughout this book, you will experience all sorts of people. Running a Bed and Breakfast is not for the faint-hearted.

Warning notices

Worn steps and loose tiles are an obvious danger, no matter how used you have become to avoiding them yourself. Many lovely old houses have steps or floors that are uneven, worn down by the tramping of feet over many years. Put up a small sign to warn your guest. Mend the loose tiles, there is no excuse for those. Low beams and archways lend character to old properties, but are less attractive when you hit your head on them. Put an amusing warning notice where the guest can see it in time. That is all you need to do, don't become neurotic with worry. You have obviously taken the care needed to warn guests of a hazard. After that, it's up to them.

PARKING

Private parking is a huge bonus to a Bed and Breakfast. If you've got it, flaunt it. I have found occasionally that people completely lose interest in making a booking when they discover I cannot offer them on-site parking. The parking situation is certainly something that I consider very important when I am booking up a Bed and Breakfast for myself.

If you cannot provide your own parking, and many small Bed and Breakfasts will not be able to, make sure you are familiar with the parking regulations in the streets around your house, and in the nearest public car park. Guests will ask for your advice on the best place to park. If you are discussing this subject on the phone when they book, take the opportunity to suggest that they stop outside your house, provided this is possible, to unload luggage, family or the dog, before they go off in search of a parking slot. This will make life easier for them, saving possible frayed tempers after a long journey.

CYCLISTS

Cyclists are great users of small Bed and Breakfasts. They will not stay with you however unless you can provide safe storage for their bicycles. This is most important to them. You can provide it in your garage, your shed or even under strong plastic sheeting, provided it is in a secure garden. Make sure you have some of this plastic sheeting always available if this is what you are going to offer. It is not expensive and can be bought in rolls from a builder's merchant. You will find it has many other uses, besides being clean and easy protection for bicycles.

I have always found cyclists to be the nicest of guests. I have met many as I am on the route from John o'Groats to Land's End, which is a popular cycling challenge. I do not mind making the effort to work out the best place for their bicycles. I always find it interesting to watch them load and unload their machines. It is really quite extraordinary how much gear these serious long distance riders can manage to carry. No wonder they are grateful if I offer to put a load through the washing machine for them. (It then dries on the hot towel rail in their bathroom.)

As a last resort, you could offer to store bicycles in another room in your house. These could stand on a piece of your useful plastic sheeting to save the floor. They will be gone first thing in the morning. Make the effort, cyclists are almost always lovely people to have to stay.

FACILITIES FOR DISABLED GUESTS

Another thing that you will have to consider is whether you have suitable facilities for disabled guests to stay at your Bed and Breakfast. You may not think that your house is suitable for wheelchair guests, but sometimes facilities can be provided without too much trouble or expense. For instance, a few steps can be overcome with a moveable wooded ramp. Grab rails in the shower are a sensible idea anyway, not just for disabled guests.

If you are a small business and it would be disproportionately expensive or downright impossible to provide facilities for disabled guests, then there is no law at present that can force you to provide the necessary facilities to include disabled guests. Many attractive Bed and Breakfast businesses will have to close if such a law does come into being. Your house may for instance have only one entrance, and that might be up a flight of steps rising steeply up from a narrow pavement. You may have no suitable ground floor rooms, or if you have, these may be too small to be adapted, or have very narrow doorways.

Remember, however, that people with disabilities often travel in company with friends or helpers. These people, with your cooperation as well, may be able to overcome any minor difficulties with your accommodation. When you accept the booking you must be sure to explain exactly what the limitations of your house are, and what you can offer in the way of help. This way you may well get to meet some wonderful people, and there will be no misunderstandings or disappointment on either side.

So now you have thought about the house you are living in, and whether it will turn itself into a successful Bed and Breakfast. Or maybe you have already decided to move out and find yourself the perfect house in the perfect location. Before making your final decision about whether your current house is suitable as a Bed and Breakfast here are some points to consider:

- ◆ Realistically calculate the cost of carrying out any alterations, whether they are to give you privacy and/or to comply with health and safety requirements.

- ◆ Remember that ancillary buildings can sometimes be turned into letting rooms.

- ◆ Be sure you know about local parking regulations.

- ◆ Think about where you could provide safe storage for bicycles.

- ◆ Work out whether you could provide some or all facilities needed by disabled guests.

Part Two

Preparing to Start and Run your Bed and Breakfast

4

Equipping Your Bed and Breakfast

GETTING ORGANISED

W ell, you are still reading the book, so it looks like you have considered everything that is involved in running a successful, small Bed and Breakfast in your own home, and you're going to go for it. Yes? Good for you!

Now you have a busy time ahead, planning for the arrival of your first guests. Get into the habit of making lists. Note down everything that has to be done, large and small. It is so satisfying when you can cross things off as having been completed. It is better to use a notebook rather than scraps of paper that will disappear. Be orderly and set out jobs for that day, and jobs for longer term. Stick to the list, working through it methodically. Do the worst jobs first to get them out of the way, then you can enjoy the others.

Keeping receipts

Get organised. Setting up your business correctly right at the start will mean there is less to go wrong later. Have a large, clearly marked filing envelope ready to slip in every receipt you receive for the work you are doing to set up the business, or the equipment you are having to buy – linen, cutlery, fire alarm, extra door keys, coat hangers. KEEP EVERY RECEIPT. No matter how small, it all adds up. Many of these will be needed when you come to offset the cost of setting up your business against the tax you will have to pay on the profit you make. Keeping receipts for everything connected to your Bed and Breakfast is essential. Get into the habit of keeping them safe. An even more efficient idea is to keep all receipts filed in monthly order. That will make things much easier when you come to deal with your accountant later. You will need an accountant initially because they are so good at showing you what you can offset against your profit (see page 120 for more on this).

GUEST BEDROOMS

First impression

Start off by taking a long critical look at the bedrooms that you have decided to dedicate to guest use. Would you be pleased to be shown into one of them if you were the guest? Are they bright and welcoming, or are they rather dated and dreary? Do they make you feel tired and flat, or do your spirits rise as you look around at the attractive decor and pictures, and take in the comfortable-looking bed, with its pretty bedspread? Are they furnished with just exactly what a guest needs for a temporary stay, or are they stuffed full of unwanted furniture left over from the rest of the house? Are the pictures on the wall interesting or just boring? Are there any pictures at all? Is this where you have hung your old school photograph or that dreary needlepoint piece that you inherited years ago? Neither of these will enliven the room for your paying guest.

You can set about putting all this right. Remove from the room anything that is superfluous. The room will immediately appear larger. If something is missing, like a bedside table, a chest of drawers, writing table and chair, take a look around your house to see what could be used. Do not rush out to buy new immediately. Strong wooden chairs can look wonderful with a bright new coat of paint. So do cheap little cabinets, which can be transformed into bedside tables or bookcases.

Charity shops

Make full use of the things you can find in charity shops or your recycling outlet. These recycling outlets, where you can buy discarded goods, are increasing in number around the country. Many of them sell very good furniture at a fraction of the shop price, as well as everything else under the sun. Lots of useful items for your Bed and Breakfast can be found there if you use your imagination, and learn to be handy at repairs and restoring. A new set of handles or knobs can work wonders, so can paint and polish.

Windows

Take a look at the windows in the room. These must be easy to keep clean. Find a reliable window cleaner, or buy yourself one of those extendable sponge mops that are designed to reach up to windows from the outside. Make cleaning the inside of your windows one of your regular chores.

Be sure to look regularly inside any secondary double glazing to check that the woodwork is clean. This area can become mildewy, and there are always dead flies in here which need to be cleaned out.

Do the windows open easily? Guests always seem to want to fling their windows open wide. Most DIY books will explain to you how to take out old-fashioned sash windows to replace the damaged cord which stops them moving up and down easily, or else allows them to crash down and trap your fingers. Sometimes it is simply a matter of regularly smoothing the running grooves with a stick of beeswax or soap. You should make sure that the window ledge on the outside is not covered in crusty blistering paint. If it is, give it a quick rub with sandpaper and a coat of paint. If you have window boxes on upper floor windows, the flowers in them will look wonderful from the bedroom inside, but do make sure the heavy box of earth and plants is securely attached to the sill. You do not want it crashing down into the street below.

Privacy

Now, think how you are going to provide your guest with privacy and darkness.

Some first floor rooms suffer from intrusive light coming in from street lighting outside, which will keep your guests awake at night. You may not be aware of this if you sleep on the next floor up, or at the back of the house. This problem is easily solved by sewing blackout fabric lining on to the head of existing curtains. This fabric, easily obtainable in fabric shops, is a pale grey colour and quite heavy. It will also improve the hang of the curtains.

Slatted blinds look really good, provided you remember to dust them regularly. Roman blinds also look attractive but you must remember that guests will probably be rougher with any sort of blinds than you would be, as well as less patient when the strings become tangled. You may find you are untangling impossibly twisted strings as the next guest is ringing the doorbell. It is safer to stick to curtains! You should make sure these are cleaned regularly, so they never smell musty. Never allow them to become unhooked and droopy. Curtains should be generously full, not just scraped across the window, and certainly should not be faded leftovers from another room in the house.

Check that the windows are not overlooked. If they are, you may need to provide net curtains as well, for your guests' privacy. If you don't like the stiffness of conventional net curtains, try making floaty net curtains out of white muslin. Make them fairly full, and you will give a lovely soft, misty appearance to the window. All net or muslin curtains must be regularly washed. They are not attractive in a shade of grey.

Flooring in the bedroom

The bedroom floor is important. If there is a carpet, this must be clean and unstained. This means it will need to be replaced more often than you might expect, in a room which is getting a lot of use (and bringing you an income). If you are buying new, it is sensible to choose a carpet that will not show every mark. Make sure the carpet is well-laid, with no loose bits to trip up the guests, particularly near the door.

If you already have wooden or laminate floors, these are ideal. They are so easy to keep clean, and are very robust. You should remember though, that if you use rugs on wood or laminate floors, it is essential that you fix safety webbing on the back of each one. This webbing is available in carpet shops and is economical to use. It will prevent the rugs from sliding around and possibly causing your guest to have a nasty fall. The same rule applies to rugs laid on a stone floor. So take a look at any loose rugs laid in any part of your house that the guest will have access to and get the safety webbing securely fixed on to the back of them.

Bedroom furniture

Now that you have removed the obviously rubbishy or unsuitable furniture from the room, take a look at what is left. This needs to be in good condition. Flimsy cupboards that could topple forward are not recommended, but it will probably be quite easy to attach a wooden block to the wall and screw through the back of the cupboard to secure it. Remember my great aunt's experience with her fur coat. Don't let this happen to your guests. Drawers and cupboard doors that stick must be sorted out. Remember you can rub soap or a stick of beeswax on the area of a chest of drawers where the drawer is catching on its runners, and it should relieve the problem.

Antiques

Your guests may not respect any valuable antique pieces of furniture you provide in the bedroom. Many of them might not even recognise antiques when they see them. So do not risk putting anything irreplaceable or precious to you in the guest bedrooms. Antique mirrors might look most attractive, but the mirror part is usually marked, and some guests might just think this is shabby. I had one guest who complained about the lovely, old mirror in the room. She said it was 'fly spotted' and a disgrace. After that, I stuck to new mirrors. Some people just have no appreciation of old things.

Make sure you are not providing anything that could collapse under a heavy weight. The furniture could be damaged, or even worse, the guest. Think about the use for every piece of furniture in the room, and avoid overcrowding. This room cannot be a repository for furniture that is not wanted in other parts of the house. Get rid of it.

Drawer liners

You should line all the drawers. The best thing to use for this job is odd rolls of reduced price wallpaper. Wallpaper is thick and strong and comes in some lovely designs. The base of a cupboard, even if it is intended just for shoes, can also be greatly improved by fitting in an old piece of carpet or lino.

All these minor details will add up to the general appearance and comfort of the room.

The bed

The most important item in the room is the bed. Is it in good condition? It does not matter which type of mattress you have, it will be impossible to please everyone. If you are buying new, the best you can do is to provide a general purpose, middle-of-the-road mattress. This should be turned regularly according to the manufacturer's instructions. Replace it long before it becomes worn and saggy in the middle. Protect it with a mattress protector, which must be regularly washed.

Pillows

It is probably better to buy new pillows. Provide a minimum of two pillows for each guest. Don't be tempted to put lumpy old pillows into new pillow slips and think that your guests will not notice. They will. Choose non-feather pillows because people can be allergic to feathers. They are cheaper to replace, and easier to clean, therefore more hygienic. You can keep two feather pillows in the cupboard, so guests can use them if they want a feather pillow. (I would love to find a feather pillow in the cupboard, as I much prefer them to man-made fibre.)

Duvets

For the same reason, choose non-feather duvets as well. They are far cheaper to replace, and easy to wash. If you want to offer the luxury of down duvets, and these are indeed marvellously warm and light, be prepared to provide a non-feather duvet if requested.

As a child sleeping in an unheated bedroom under those heavy blankets, like those used to keep horses warm, I was delighted when I went to Germany and first came across duvets. This was the early 1950s and these wonders were unheard of on this side of the Channel. Sleeping in them was like lying under heated thistledown. No wonder they became universally popular. I have found people surprisingly fussy about bedding. Having the spare feather pillows and duvet will mean that in theory you will be able to please everyone – except those who want a sheet with blankets.

Blankets

I have very occasionally been asked, both at the time of booking and on arrival, if the bed can be made up with a sheet and blankets. People want what they are used to, so try to oblige if possible.

If you supply blankets, stored in a plastic cover in the cupboard against the possibility of a really cold spell, these will probably never be used. However, guests seem to like the security of knowing they are there, just in case. Even if they may never be used, make sure they are clean and smell fresh. Do avoid the heavy old-fashioned ones. Send these off for use in colder countries where they will be appreciated. You can also supply a nice warm throw at the end of the bed, or over a chair. Scattering a few soft cushions on the bed makes it look more inviting.

Room temperature

You should check the temperature in the bedroom. How reliable is the central heating radiator in the room? Is it going to be warm enough? Your guest should be able to control the temperature. It is not advisable to use any fires with exposed flames or bars, or any type of heater that could be knocked over. Any heater that you are using should be firmly attached to the wall or floor.

I have found it a wise precaution to keep an electric convector heater available for each of my letting rooms. This is against the day the boiler fails me in cold weather. These emergency heaters need not be stored in the guest bedroom, just have them stored somewhere handy to produce if needed. Be sure you buy the type with fail safe devices that turn off immediately, if the heater is knocked over. I do not advocate using these to heat the rooms on a regular basis, just to keep in case of emergency. Likewise, have an immersion heater installed for emergency hot water. You may well never need these precautions, but you will be very glad of them if the need does arise.

LINEN

You will need to stock up on bed linen and towels. Do not be mean about this. It is sensible to have at least one complete change for each bed. It is best to stick to the one colour, probably white, but this is your personal choice. Having enough linen will prevent a panic during busy periods when you are rushing to get washed and aired linen back on the beds before the arrival of the next guest. If you have a mixed variety of respectable linen and towels, there is nothing wrong in using these up for your first couple of years of business. Always remember that your washing machine and dryer are quite capable of letting you down at the least convenient time. You should find out where your local launderette is, and what sort of service it offers, in case you ever need it.

You will need the following for each bed:

◆ a mattress protector
◆ bottom sheet (I prefer flat to fitted – so much easier to iron)
◆ duvet cover

- inner pillow slips
- outer pillow slips.

It is currently the fashion to provide an additional layer on top of the mattress, under the bottom sheet. These mattress toppers provide lovely extra luxury. I have never bought custom-made toppers; I find that elderly duvets do the job just as well. These must be the synthetic, easily washable type of duvet, of course.

Sometimes you will find a Bed and Breakfast that provides a sheet between you and the duvet. This is a strange thing to do, because the idea of a duvet is that it moulds itself to your body, and a sheet just gets in the way. I suspect it is a way of avoiding washing the more awkward duvet covers. I am happier to know that the duvet cover has been washed fresh for each guest. Using the sheet method could tempt you to be lazy in this respect.

A suitable bedspread will finish off your bed. It should match the room decor, and must be washable. A grubby bedspread is a real turn off for guests.

Laundering

The necessary frequent washing of guest linen and towels in a busy Bed and Breakfast will take its toll. Towels in particular can soon become thin and tired looking. Guests will spill wine, tea and cosmetics on the bed just like the rest of us. You will find there are bargains in bed linen and towels to be found during the sales, as well as shops that specialise in permanent discounts. Just remember, when you are buying discontinued lines cheaply, you are not likely to be able to match up designs later.

Towels

It is important to provide nice fluffy towels. I put out a bath towel and a smaller hand towel for each guest. I leave a pile of clean fluffy flannels in the bathroom. Check your towels and replace them when they start looking worn, and always if they have become stained or damaged.

I do not think it matters what colour the towels are, but if they are white, you must make sure they are really white, not a dingy grey colour. To fluff up towels you need to soak them in warm water and Borax, before washing them on the warm cycle of your machine. Giving them a final dry off in the tumble dryer after drying them outside will also improve the feel of towels. Some landladies replace the towels daily, but as we are all trying to save the planet by washing less frequently, I think fresh towels every day is too much of a luxury, unless of course they are dirty rather than just damp. Let damp ones dry off on the heated bathroom towel rail.

I consider that heated towel rails are essential in a guest bathroom. They will heat up the room, and guests will use them to dry off small bits of washing. Buy the biggest towel rail you can afford, some have the dual ability to work off either the central heating or by electricity.

Iron and ironing board

I supply an ironing board and an iron in a cupboard on the landing for my guests. This will hopefully prevent them ironing clothes on the floor and burning the carpet, or asking to borrow my iron and board just when I am settling down to work through a pile of newly dried bed linen.

On the subject of ironing, buy yourself the widest board you can find, right at the start of the opening of your business. It will be expensive, but well worth the outlay. You will find the endless ironing of bed linen so much easier. One of those reservoir steam irons that you do not have to keep filling, and which give a real blast of steam, would be a great asset too. Don't forget both these items are tax deductible (so long as you keep the receipt)!

Items for guest use
I put a torch, hair dryer and a hot water bottle in the room, as well as a regularly updated folder with details of local events and attractions. I also leave out a current copy of the county magazine. If you are going to supply a magazine, make sure these are kept up to date. I also supply a well-stocked hospitality tray (see page 87 for more on this).

If there is room, a writing table and chair are always appreciated. Many people need a space to work on their laptops, as well as write postcards.

I also put a television set and a DVD player in each room.

Lighting
One thing that is very important in a guest bedroom is the lighting. This particularly applies to the bedside light. It is not acceptable to have to struggle to read by a low wattage bulb in a wrongly positioned lamp. Most of us grew out of reading by torchlight years ago. Try to find bedside lights that really do supply adequate light, rather than just prettily matching the decor of the room.

You can use decorative lamps around the room to provide an intimate and cosy feel to the room. Make sure these are lit, and the curtains drawn, when you are going to show a guest into the room on a winter evening. It will make the room most inviting.

Books and DVDs

The bedroom will be more welcoming and homely if you can fit in a bookshelf, with a selection of books. Try to cater for all tastes. There is no need to buy new books, and anyway these will disappear regularly. They can be quickly replaced from charity shops. I always supply a small stack of DVDs, especially a few for children. These are always popular, and will also occasionally vanish. Guests with fractious children appreciate being able to pop in a DVD for them to snuggle down and watch, while their parents unpack and make a cup of tea after a long journey.

Coat hangers

Guests will need somewhere to hang clothes, as well as a chest of drawers. At the very least if you have no hanging space, provide hooks on the back of the door, and several good quality coat hangers. Never use those flimsy wire hangers from the dry cleaners, even when they are hidden in a cupboard. They will cheapen the look of the room immediately.

Decoration

Stand back and take a look at the decoration in your letting bedrooms. If there is wallpaper this will look lovely until it becomes damaged. Then it is difficult to repair effectively, and will quickly start to look scruffy. Before this happens you can cover it with a coat of emulsion paint, which is so easy to refresh every year or so. You can dab on a quick covering for any dirty mark or scratch as it appears. Many of the modern emulsions allow you to scrub them gently, in particularly dirty spots. Keep leftover emulsion, tightly sealed, ready to touch up bad patches.

The colour scheme for your letting rooms is your choice but I do recommend that you keep it simple and impersonal. Keep wild vibrant wall colours for your own rooms. You could use large bright prints for the walls, these often look better than smaller pictures dotted around. Small pictures grouped together on a wall make something interesting to look at. Prints only need to be framed in clip frames. Do not risk putting valuable paintings on the walls of a letting room, these are too easily slipped into a suitcase. Do not hang a heavy picture over the pillow where your guest will lay his head to sleep, unless you are sure that it could not possibly fall off the wall.

Above all, everything must be very clean with no chipped paint, missing knobs or unravelling hems. I think ornaments are unnecessary. They can get broken and they certainly collect dust.

Family photos

I would always avoid putting into a letting room anything that is personal, like your family photographs or anything that has personal value to you. You may not wish to get involved with guests in a conversation about yourself or your family, so do not put photos of yourself, or them, into guest rooms.

Teddy bears

There is a trend these days to sit a teddy bear on the bed. Personally, I think this looks like something a child has left behind. Teddies and other soft animals look out of place in a letting bedroom. Guests will bring their own if they cannot be without a cuddly toy around them.

BATHROOM

Now, take a critical look at the bathroom you are providing for your guests. Whatever style this room is, whether quaintly old fashioned or streamlined ultra modern, it must be cleaner than clean. The tiles should not be damaged, or have any discoloured mouldy grout around them. These areas can usually be effectively cleaned by scrubbing with bleach. Sometimes it is necessary to cover a bad area with wadded up tissues soaked in bleach. Remove the tissues a few hours later and the area should be clean. If this does not work, or if the area is difficult to cover in this way, the damaged areas will have to be scraped out and replaced with fresh grouting.

The bath, basin and toilet should all be in good condition. These must not be chipped or stained. Do not buy cheap toilet seats, as these are not robust enough. Always supply a generous number of toilet rolls. Avoid buying the really cheap variety.

Bathroom flooring

Carpet on the bathroom floor is not the best idea, as it smells once it becomes damp. The best floor covering is tiles or lino, both of which can be quickly washed and dried off. Sometimes you can expose and paint wooden floorboards, which look very effective. These can be quickly repainted with quick-drying floor paint to keep them looking fresh. You will need to be careful in your choice of bathmat as these can slip as a guest steps out of the bath. Use rubber backed mats, or put non-slip backing strips on the underside of the mat. You can provide a lightweight bathmat, freshly laundered for each changeover, to go on top of a more robust mat that has non-slip backing.

USING THE CASH AND CARRY

You will need to register with your local cash and carry bulk buy store. These are usually sited on industrial estates on the outskirts of town. You can send them a copy of your brochure to obtain a card that enables you to shop there.

Cash and carry stores do not offer huge value to a small Bed and
Breakfast, but they are the only stockists of single serving packs
of sugar, coffee, biscuits and soap. They are also the stockists for
those single portions of long-life milk. You will need these for the
hospitality trays in your bedrooms. You may prefer to supply a
jar of instant coffee, a small airtight jar of biscuits, a bowl of
sugar and a flask of fresh milk for your guests. This all provides
a very nice touch, but will be harder work than providing the pre-
packed ingredients from the cash and carry. You will have to
judge what to do when you know what sort of guests are going to
be using your rooms.

The cash and carry will also have individual packets of shampoo,
conditioner and body lotion. You will have to decide what you
are going to offer your guests. I keep a small basket in the
bathroom filled with individual shampoos and conditioners, but I
find these are very seldom used. In fact, I have to make sure they
do not become dusty! Guests always seem to bring their own. I
supply a small soap dispenser for the basin, as this can be refilled
and hygienically used again and again. I put out a selection of
bars of soap for the bath, but again I find guests usually prefer to
provide their own. Once any soap has been opened, I use it up
myself. You can also put out a bowl of individual soaps from the
cash and carry. These will look more attractive if you can get a
mix of colours. Again, I use these up myself, being an economical
sort of person. Never leave out a used bar of soap for a guest on
their first day with you. Obviously if they are staying more than
one day, they use the same soap.

If you provide refillable containers of any product in the bathroom,
make sure they contain exactly what is stated on the container.
Otherwise guests with allergies may be affected, and blame you.

So I hope I have now given you an idea of what you will have to provide to equip your Bed and Breakfast. I hope I have also shown you the most economical way to do this. Here are some points to remember:

- Look critically at the bedroom and bathroom from the guest's point of view.

- Check the state of the windows, curtains and carpets; always use non-slip safety backing on rugs laid on anything but carpet.

- Check that all furniture is suitable and robust.

- Do not over furnish.

- Remember that the bed and mattress are very important items.

- Make sure the room heating can be controlled by the guest.

- Buy sufficient linen and towels.

- Check the bedside lighting is adequate for reading in bed.

- Check that the wall decoration can be easily maintained.

- Check that the bathroom is easy to keep clean and replace any damaged fittings.

5

The Day-to-Day Running of a Bed and Breakfast

BEING READY WHEN THE GUEST ARRIVES

The unbreakable golden rule that applies to the successful running of a small Bed and Breakfast is that you should always be ready for the arrival of your guests. By this I mean that you must not find that you are running off in search of clean towels, or that the vacuum cleaner is sitting in the middle of the guest bedroom, when the doorbell rings.

You should get into the habit from the start of always cleaning and preparing the guest rooms immediately after the previous guest has left. You should do this even if no one is expected immediately. You never know when you will get a chance to take in a guest. Learn to be ready for these chances, this is how you will make money. The only exception to everything being ready in the room is the vase of fresh flowers. Even the smallest vase will look welcoming to the guest. I find that chrysanthemums are very good value. You can break off the little sprigs and from these you can make up several small vases from one not very expensive bunch of long-lasting chrysanthemums.

Keeping the house smelling fresh

If your rooms have been empty for a while, you should quickly wipe down the paintwork with a fresh smelling cleaning product. You can also give a well kept and welcoming feel to a room by polishing any wood surface with a scented wax polish. The smell lingers in the air.

Remember not to paint, cook curry, fish or garlic chutney when you are expecting guests to arrive. The house will smell very strongly of these odours. This is a rule of course for when you are actually expecting guests. If guests arrive on the off chance of a room, all you can do is apologise for the strong smell and open some windows. They will be grateful to have found somewhere to sleep for the night. It is better to keep these strong smelling activities for when you know you are having a time free of guests.

There are plug-in or spray-on products that create a smell of sea breezes or spring flowers, but be careful not to overuse these. You do not want your guest to suspect you of hiding more sinister smells. These products should not be used as a short cut to thorough cleaning. If you like the artificial fragrance – I don't – they are best kept for the hall or the bathroom.

Being prepared for the unexpected

The very first time I admitted guests into my newly opened first Bed and Breakfast, it was a wet and windy Devon afternoon. The doorbell rang and a family group were huddled on the doorstep, wanting to get out of the wet. I was not actually expecting guests quite so soon, although once they were there on the doorstep, I was not going to turn them away. My very first guests!

But there was one problem. The plumber needed a further half-hour to finish off his work. So I produced a tray of tea, and plenty of chocolate biscuits. Just in the nick of time the plumber announced that he had finished. Unfortunately, it was soon clear that he had become flustered at the unexpected hurry. He had somehow managed to attach the toilet cistern to the hot water supply. The result was the ultimate hot flush! Luckily, my guests were amused, and it was all quickly sorted out.

On another occasion I took in a party of young German walkers, on an equally wet afternoon. I did not have enough beds for them all. The weather was so foul that they were determined not to go back out into it, so they accepted the rooms I did have. Then, they worked out an ingenious distribution of bedding and mattresses, borrowing some sofa cushions from me. The next morning everything was put back into its place before they left. They were quite happy to pay my normal charge, and one of that group came back to stay several more times.

Be flexible about the needs of your guests. Go with the flow when necessary.

Fresh flowers in the bedroom

Fresh flowers in the bedroom are always a winner, so long as you replace them the minute they begin to wilt. If you cannot get fresh flowers, put a flowering plant in their place. Be careful to avoid flowers with pollen that stains clothing, or flowers with a really cloying scent. The simple act of putting out a vase of fresh flowers shows that you have made an effort to welcome your guest. Artificial flowers somehow just manage to make a room look tired and dated. They also attract dust, which makes them look even worse.

ARRIVAL OF GUESTS

If you are registered with your local TIC be prepared for phone calls around tea time. This is when people decide that they must find a place to spend the night. The TIC will send the guests round to you once you have accepted the booking, so that is why you need to be ready for them. Sometimes guests use a mobile phone to book while they are sitting outside your house in the car. This is not the moment to remember that you have not yet cleaned the bathroom after the last guest's departure.

Get into the habit of keeping any doors which lead into the private areas of your house firmly closed. There is no reason why you should keep your private rooms immaculate, but do keep your family clutter hidden from guests. There is also no point in advertising to guests any antiques or valuables that you own.

I always show my guests to their room, rather than pointing up the stairs and saying: 'First on the right!'

If you offer a tray of tea and biscuits when your guest arrives, even better home-made cake, it will go a long way towards breaking the ice, and make a good start to their stay with you. This is more relevant with guests who are planning a longer stay, rather than the single night bookings. You will soon learn to recognise the guests who will respond to this treatment, and which guests would much rather be left on their own as soon as possible. Do not force yourself on to guests. Stay long enough in the room to show them where various things are, and don't forget to tell them when and where you will be serving breakfast. Remember to make sure that you know if they are vegetarians or vegans.

Breakfast time
I am flexible about the time I serve breakfast. I am used to engineers staying with me who have to make a very early start. But I am also happy to do late breakfasts for those who want it, provided this will fit into my next guest's arrival time. Most people expect to eat breakfast between 8 a.m. and 9 a.m. If your guest has not made any sound when the agreed time for breakfast has arrived, give a discreet knock on the door.

Front door keys

I always give my guests a key to the front door. I never give them the second key which double locks the door when I am away, and which I seldom use otherwise. You may not feel happy about giving your guests a key to the front door of your house. If you decide this is the case then you will have to be prepared to let guests in and out whenever they choose to come and go. Guests expect to come in and out of the house at will; they seldom just disappear off for the whole day.

Although I always give a key, I never go to bed myself before the last guest is home for the night. Then, I lock up. This is also a sure way of knowing that you have only the number of guests who are paying to stay with you!

Copying keys

Of course there is always the risk that guests can, if they want to, get the key copied. They can then return yours at the end of the stay, and retain a copy of your door key. There is not much you can do about this possibility, except NEVER give out keys to your mortise lock. This is the lock you use when you go away from home on holiday, or when you are on your own with no guests coming in and out of the house. Just a sensible precaution.

I once gave a family group their key, and I was given back three. They had found it easier to get the key copied, so that they had one each, than to ask me for two extra keys! I assume they were honest, and I got two free keys.

If you decide to give up running a Bed and Breakfast, it would be sensible to change the lock that your guests have been using. Again, just a precaution.

Guests who have been drinking

A problem you may have is the guest who has been drinking, and on his return cannot remember which is his bedroom. This does happen. You should remember that some people travel all over the country, staying at a different Bed and Breakfast each night. They cannot remember the layout of each house.

I once had a group of hard working, hard drinking engineers who were barely able to find the front door, let alone the keyhole. They used to finish work at four, after a very early start, and go straight to the pub. This sounds alarming, but, in fact, these were respectful and pleasant men, far from home, and only needing a bit of good-tempered banter and guidance to find their own rooms. My only worry was that one of them (the heaviest drinker) always wanted to say goodnight to the dog. I always worried that he would fall asleep with the dog under the table before I could persuade him up to his room.

A broad-minded attitude and a good sense of humour are essential to a landlady on these occasions.

Curfew for guests

I suppose you can make a curfew for your guests. But could you enforce it? Would you really want an irate guest banging on your locked front door in the dead of night? It is much better to wait up and see them all safely in. You will not have to do this often.

Bedroom locks

Guests expect to be able to lock their bedroom doors when they are inside their room. Locks are not always easy to fit, especially on old doors. I settled on fitting those chain locks that are designed to prevent anyone pushing their way in, and they are not complicated to fit. This seems to me to be a good compromise for a small Bed and Breakfast. If you have visiting children, or your own, who lock themselves in the room, it is easy to speak and see through the door. And in an emergency you can cut the chain. These locks have never been commented on by my guests so I assume they meet with approval. I have the same chain lock on my own bedroom door. I never fail to lock my door, however well I think I know my guests.

TAKING BOOKINGS

You will soon get used to handling bookings over the phone. I always use my own personal diary for bookings, because then I can instantly see if I have any other commitments, as well as other bookings. I may not want to be committed to guests on that date. If you do not keep a diary, or want to use a dedicated bookings book, then choose a hard backed diary that displays one week at a glance.

You should always know where this book is, or where your personal diary is, so that you can refer to it quickly. It is embarrassing to keep a potential guest waiting on the phone while you frantically hunt around. It is also embarrassing to have to call back and cancel a booking that you have just accepted, because you find you have double booked.

Keeping a record of guests

It is essential to take an address and a contact phone number from the guest. A mobile phone number is useful so you can contact the guest if it gets very late and you want to know if in fact the guest is planning to come. I usually find that guests who are delayed will telephone me, but if it is me that calls them, they are always grateful to hear that the room is still waiting for them.

It is also important to keep a file record of all guest addresses and phone contacts, and their booking dates. This means that if something happens to you, say illness or family emergency, you will be able to ask a friend to contact the guests, even if you cannot do this yourself. Guests may be annoyed to be cancelled, but they will be much more annoyed to arrive at an empty house with you in the local hospital.

If you provide evening meals, mention this at the time of the booking, and suggest a menu and a time for the meal to be served.

Confirming bookings

I always confirm a booking, provided there is time to do this. This is not possible if the guest is arriving the next day. But if I can do it, I enclose my brochure, so that guests can get a fuller picture of my Bed and Breakfast facilities before they arrive. Always keep a copy of this confirmation letter on file.

There is an example of a letter (on page 82) written to a fictitious Mrs Daisy Jones, confirming her booking. She has made the booking on a Monday evening, and is arriving on the Thursday, so there is no time for her to send me a cheque as deposit.

Head the letter with your name, address, phone number, mobile number, email address and website. Don't forget to put the date.

Make sure that you keep a copy of the letter you have written to Mrs Jones, and that you have made a note of her telephone number on the letter, and in your bookings book. That way, if you have to contact her, or someone else has to do this, the number is quickly available.

Mrs Daisy Jones

18 Springfield Avenue

Southsea

Hampshire P05 8ZP

Dear Mrs Jones

Thank you for your phone call today to book one double room with two single beds for the nights of 23 and 24 July 2008, for yourself and your 12-year-old daughter.

I note that you will be arriving around 6 p.m., and that you will be bringing with you one small dog.

The charge for the room will be £25 per night for yourself, and £15 per night for your daughter, making a total payment of £80. I also make a charge of £2 per night for dogs.

I am enclosing a copy of my brochure for your information. Please note that I do not accept credit cards. I would be grateful to receive payment on your arrival.

I look forward to meeting you both. If your plans change, I would be most grateful if you would telephone to let me know.

Yours sincerely,

Christabel Milner

Of course, as I do not take credit cards, I will have no way of charging Mrs Jones if she does not turn up to take the room. But I have found over many years that this seldom happens (twice in 20 years), so I would not worry about it. I am sure Mrs Jones will phone if she is either going to be very much later than she says, or for some reason she cannot come, so there will at least be a slight chance of re-letting her room.

The letter on page 84 is to a fictitious Kelly Johnson, who has telephoned to tell me that she is getting married on 12 June in the local church. She is young, friendly and excited, and uses my first name, so I use hers in my reply. You have to judge when to do this, and when to be more formal. She has asked me how near my house is to the church and to the country club where she is holding her reception. She wants to reserve a room for her parents and her brother.

Head the letter with your name, address, phone number, mobile number, email address and website. Don't forget the date.

If Kelly's deposit cheque does not arrive within a few days, I shall phone her to remind her to send it as soon as possible. If it still fails to arrive, and another booking comes in for the same day I am afraid I shall take the second booking. I shall write and tell Kelly that I am no longer holding her booking. I do think people need to be business-like about these things. If she wants the room for her parents and brother, she will send the cheque (or get them to). I feel pretty sure I shall receive the money as she sounded very genuine. But you never know.

Payment by card

You should make sure that your brochure states whether you

Kelly Johnson
Flat 6
24 Harrow Road
London SE19 5AP

Dear Kelly

Thank you for your telephone call today.

I have reserved a double-bedded room for the nights of 12 and 13 June 2008, for your parents, John and Mary Johnson. I have also reserved a single room for your brother and I note he will be staying just the night of 12 June.

I am enclosing a copy of my brochure. Please note that I do not accept credit cards.

As we discussed, my charges are £25 per adult per night, so that will be a total of £100 for your parents and £25 for your brother. I note that you will be sending me a 10% deposit of £12.50 within the next few days to secure this booking.

There will be no problem about your parents arriving as early as 11 a.m. on 12 June in order to have time to change for your wedding.

I shall also be pleased to provide an evening meal for your parents on 13 June, and I will discuss the menu with them when they arrive.

St Peter's Church is about five minutes' walk from my house, and the Carlisle Country Club is about fifteen minutes by car. The local taxi firm is 01769 600000 if you need to book taxis for any of your guests. I would advise you to do this soon.

I look forward to meeting your family, and I hope you have a wonderful day.

Yours sincerely,

Christabel Milner

accept credit cards. I do not accept these as there are three banks with cashpoints within walking distance of my house, not to mention the number of other outlets for obtaining cash. Making it clear from the beginning that you do not accept payment by card will avoid misunderstandings. Always mention it on the phone, and in your confirmation letter, if you have time to send one. Failing all this, mention it to the guest on arrival.

Making verbal contact

I do not take bookings from email contact only. I always prefer to speak directly to the person who is booking the room if I possibly can. That way you can learn something about them, as well as establishing that your Bed and Breakfast is going to suit their needs. In a larger establishment where there are staff, or where at least there are other people in the house, this is not so important. But if you live and work alone, this verbal contact is advisable. As you become more experienced as a Bed and Breakfast landlady, you will find you can learn a lot about a person from just a telephone conversation. Of course, you can occasionally be wrong, but I have found this is not often the case.

Deciding not to accept a guest

There may be occasions when you choose to be fully booked for the dates requested by a guest who you do not like the sound of. Something about the telephone call will warn you off. You may well be wrong, but you will never know, and it is always better to be safe than sorry. Likewise, when people knock on the door wanting a room, you have to make an immediate decision about whether to take them in or not. Go with your instincts. It is always better to lose a bit of income than to find yourself alone in the house with someone you would rather not have there.

A friend of mine had a clear glass panel inserted in the front door of his Bed and Breakfast. He then had several seconds before he opened the door to form an assessment of the caller. Of course, if the person knocking is already booked with you, you are stuck with them however unpromising their appearance! Always remember that first appearances are often most deceptive. Tired, surly arrivals can become quite pleasant people after they have had a rest and a cup of tea. I am often surprised how differently guests turn out, compared to my initial impression of them.

TICs make a point of getting to know their Bed and Breakfast landladies. They will often 'filter' guests that they send you. So it is always worth getting to know the staff at your local TIC. Nothing and nobody is completely foolproof though when it comes to judging character.

Payment on arrival

This has to be done tactfully, but firmly. Your guest has booked a room, you have held the room for them and it is all ready. Why should he or she not pay you for it? You are running a business, not a charity. All hotels will insist on taking a credit card number when the booking is made. Your business is too small to do this, so politely ask for the money when the guest arrives. Any extras, like a decision to have an evening meal, or some baby- or dog-sitting that you subsequently agree to do can of course be paid for at the end of the stay.

Whenever I use a Bed and Breakfast, I always insist on paying when I arrive. I am surprised that many landladies do not ask for payment on arrival.

Of course, with regular guests that you feel you know well, you can be more relaxed.

DAILY ROOM CLEANING

When your guests are staying for several days, you will need to straighten out their rooms, and give a quick daily clean. I try not to move or touch any clothes or possessions. I change the bed linen every three or four days, and towels when necessary. Don't forget to empty the waste paper basket, and the bin in the bathroom. Lining each of these with a plastic bag will make the job easier and quicker.

Check the hospitality tray, replace dirty cups and make sure it is well stocked. The guest should not think that what is supplied on the first day is the ration for the duration of their stay. The contents of the hospitality tray are cheap enough, so by being generous you can create a good impression without it costing you too much.

Hospitality trays

Hospitality trays are expected in even the smallest Bed and Breakfasts. The minimum you should supply is:

- a cup, saucer and teaspoon for each person
- small dish for used tea bags
- coffee, tea and sugar
- whatever sort of milk you have decided to provide.

I put a small tea pot on the tray, and I also include a couple of individual packets of biscuits and a selection of fruit teas and drinking chocolate. If you use either the single sachets of long-life milk or the individual packets of biscuits be sure to note their expiry date. Note it in your bookings book and be sure to replace them. In my experience, they do not last much over that date.

Recipe for out-of-date biscuits

I have a favourite way of using up expired biscuits. I just crush a few packets into some chocolate melted in a pan with butter. I add sultanas and sometimes desiccated coconut. Press this mixture down well in a shallow tin, rubbing a cut orange firmly over the surface. Let it harden in the fridge, then cut it into bite sized pieces to eat while you are doing the ironing, or waiting up for a late night guest.

Electric kettles

In the guest bedrooms, make sure the kettle is placed near a suitable electric outlet, preferably on a hard, flat surface like a table. Replace the kettle as soon as there is any sign of wear. These are cheap enough to buy, and it is always better to be safe.

TRYING OUT THE ROOMS YOURSELF

On guest-free days, you should regularly sleep in your guest bedrooms yourself, and use their bathrooms, so you can experience what they are experiencing.

While you are lying in bed you may notice cobwebs that you have missed while cleaning. You may discover that the bedside light is in the wrong place, or that the duvet is not warm enough. When you are in the bath, you may look around and notice that the toilet brush is in too prominent a position, and that the bath water is running out too slowly. (This usually means you need to pour in a drain cleaner to clear any blockage, or merely that you have not kept the plug hole clear of accumulated hair and waste.) It may occur to you that a picture would brighten up a plain corner, or that the glass globe lampshade has dead flies trapped inside it. (It is a mystery how these flies get in, but they manage it somehow.)

SMOKING

A 'No Smoking' notice in your Bed and Breakfast brochure, bedroom or hallway will not stop determined smokers. They will try to insist that they only smoke out of an open window. This is most unlikely. You will only discover that the room smells of stale smoke when you go in to clean it the next day. By then of course the culprit is long gone. And what could you do about it anyway? All you can do is to wash everything that is washable, and throw open the windows for as long as possible before the next guest arrives. The smell of an occasional cigarette will disappear quite quickly. It is an irritation, but it will happen.

I hope I have given you some idea of the day-to-day running of a Bed and Breakfast. Be adaptable and prepared for anything, and keep your sense of humour. Here is a list of some of the points I have raised:

- Always keep the guest rooms in a state of readiness for guests.

- Keep all doors closed to rooms that are not available to guests.

- Show your guests into their rooms.

- Provide a generous hospitality tray.

- Remember that an open mind and a good sense of humour are essential.

- Confirm bookings by post or email if possible and keep a record on file.

- Always take a contact phone number for guests.

- Remember that you can always say you are fully booked.

6

Providing a Good Breakfast and an Evening Meal

After a comfortable, clean bedroom, and a well-equipped bathroom, the next most important thing about a Bed and Breakfast for the guest is the breakfast itself.

The great British breakfast is well known and loved all over the world, and you cannot go far wrong by serving a well-cooked fry up, toast and tea or coffee. But you can also add some refinements, and in these health and figure conscious days you can cut down on the calories of a traditional cooked breakfast by grilling instead of frying, wherever possible.

Not everyone wants a cooked breakfast, so it is wise to have some tasty alternatives in the form of home-made muesli, a variety of rolls, fruit salad and yoghurt.

When you have guests for several days, discuss breakfast with them. They may be perfectly happy every day with the standard fry up you have just served them, or they might like to be more adventurous and try your porridge, fried kidneys with bacon or omelettes. I steer clear of kippers, because it is difficult (but not impossible) to source good ones, and because of the smell. But if your guest has requested them, don't worry about the smell!

SERVING BREAKFAST

Crockery
I think it is a matter of personal taste what pattern of crockery

you choose for your Bed and Breakfast. Many people favour plain white, which always looks bright and clean. This looks very good against a coloured tablecloth, and breakages are easy to replace.

I have always used non-matching crockery, but this is just a personal quirk of mine. I like the cheerful and unusual appearance, and it has the added advantage that I do not have to worry when I break something, another piece can take its place, adding to the mixture. A local tea shop was recently written up in the national press as having 'a delightfully mismatched collection of china'. I was pleased to see that I have apparently been a fashion leader in this field for years!

Food safety and cleanliness

It goes without saying that everything must be clean. A dishwasher is an essential item for a Bed and Breakfast. The water is hot enough to make sure that everything is sterilised. Be sure you are storing food at the correct temperature in your fridge or freezer. Remember that you must store cooked and raw meats on separate shelves. Everything in the fridge must be covered, and the fridge itself kept very clean.

It is not yet a requirement for a small Bed and Breakfast landlady, but if you take part in a food safety and hygiene course, for which you will obtain a certificate on passing the test, you will be well prepared in the matter of food safety. Do not take any risks with food safety, throw it out if you have any doubts about anything.

Pets at mealtimes

You should always remove any pets of your own from the room

where you are serving a meal. Sometimes guests will ask you to let them stay. There are some guests who enjoy seeing the family cat or dog in its usual place. (Provided of course that such pets are guest friendly.)

Very few Bed and Breakfasts will let guests bring their pets into the room where the meal is served. They either stay up in the bedroom, or are put into the car. If the guests with the pets are your only guests at the time, of course you can please yourself what rules you make. If you are large enough to have several guests at a time, it is fair to warn the people who are bringing their animals with them what the house rules are for their pets. This way there is no bad feeling.

Fresh flowers in the breakfast room
Flowers in the room where your guests are eating brighten everything up, but do be sure to remove them the minute they begin to droop, otherwise they are just depressing.

Adapting to your guests' needs
All your attempts to provide an excellent breakfast may be in vain if you have a group like I had one year. They were really nice guys, most polite and friendly. The first day not one of them touched their freshly squeezed orange juice. The next day I tried packet juice in a glass jug. No takers.

Then I plonked a really cheap make of juice straight on to the table, unopened. This was drained dry, obviously because it was familiar. The same group explained to me that they did not want 'the full Monty' breakfast, as they described it. They always met up with their mates for a break and a fry up in a cafe later in the morning. So what could I give them? We settled on poached eggs with baked beans. I went out and bought an egg poacher, which has proved to be a most useful item.

'Them lovely little round eggs!' was their description. Everyone was happy!

What makes a good breakfast

Breakfast is my favourite meal, so I really enjoy cooking and presenting a good one. My standard breakfast menu is as follows:

♦ freshly squeezed orange juice

♦ home-made muesli (porridge oats, wheatgerm, crushed nuts, dried coconut, sultanas, chopped dates and sliced almonds)

♦ assorted mini cereal packets

♦ fruit salad.

All the above items are set out ready for the guests to serve themselves when they come down. If I just have one or two guests, everything is out on the same table. If there are several guests, I set out these starters on a side table. I occasionally also put out yoghurts and sliced cheese, depending on the guests. Children usually love yoghurt.

Don't forget that you must warn guests if anything you provide contains nuts. I actually write this fact on the container that I use to serve my muesli, to be really safe.

I rely on tinned grapefruit, stewed prunes, sliced fresh apples and kiwi fruit in the winter for my fruit salads, but in summer it is easy to make this a riotous mix of colourful fresh fruits.

My full breakfast is all of the following, unless I have been asked to leave out something:

◆ two eggs (I always offer to poach or scramble, but usually guests want a fried egg); I always buy local free range eggs

◆ bacon – I always grill this; all my bacon is locally produced

◆ sausage – again, this is grilled, and locally sourced

◆ mushrooms – these are fried, sometimes with added finely chopped parsley, if I think this will appeal to the type of guest I have

◆ tomatoes – these are either grilled or baked in the oven

◆ fried bread – this is a great favourite, and I always fry it (usually it is just a small piece, so is not too sinful)

◆ baked beans – I always ask if the guest wants these. I am always surprised at the guests that do have them. Guests are also surprisingly fussy about where on the plate they want their beans. (I serve them direct from the pan on to the plate at the table.) Some make a space on the side, but quite a few want them poured all over everything

◆ fried potatoes – occasionally, when I have some cold potato to use up; these are very popular.

Always put out bottles of brown and tomato sauce, you will be surprised how many people will smother your beautifully presented meal with this stuff! Make sure there is plenty left in the bottle, guests do not expect to squeeze out the last reluctant drops.

Find out the night before whether your guests want a cooked breakfast, because some, though not very many, will shudder at the thought. But wait until the guest is sitting at the breakfast table before you finalise the details. Often I find that guests are not interested in discussing breakfast, they prefer to wait and be pleasantly surprised.

Vegetarians and vegans
Make sure you check whether your guests are vegans or vegetarians, or have any other dietary specialities, although people will usually (but not always) mention these themselves when they make the booking.

Remember that it is very important to use separate cooking pans and utensils when cooking for vegetarians and vegans, always keeping their food completely apart from any animal product.

Timing the meal
You will have plenty of time to cook while guests are helping themselves to what is already laid out on the table. Don't make the mistake of cooking food too early as it will just go hard and dry in the oven. People are prepared to wait for freshly cooked food. It is important to make sure that coffee or tea is served immediately the guest sits down. This should be in a tea pot or cafetière. It looks mean to offer just a cup, even if you are prepared to refill it.

If you use a cafetière for the coffee, always be sure to serve it with the plunger pushed down. If you have a guest who is not familiar with these, the resulting mess of coffee over the table will be awful. An electric coffee maker brewing on the sideboard gives a lovely smell, but of course it is then wasted if everyone orders tea.

You should make frequent offers to provide more tea, coffee or toast. The offer will almost certainly be refused, but you will appear generous.

Children will love being offered hot chocolate, served to them in their own little jug to pour out themselves. Make sure it is not too hot.

Individual portion packets

I am afraid eventually European food regulations will prevent us serving good English farmhouse butter set out attractively in a dish, but at present there is no law that insists you have to serve individual butter packets. I always serve butter, locally made if possible. I either put thin slices of this on an attractive dish, or I put it out in a neat square on a dish with a butter knife. By a neat square I mean a piece of butter cut from a new packet. Not something you have been hacking at, or something that has appeared at other meals and been cut into.

Butter or margarine

I have never been asked to substitute margarine for butter on the table. Very occasionally guests who feel strongly about the matter will produce their own pack of favoured spread. You could offer to keep this in the fridge for them if they are staying several days, or buy the same brand yourself and set it out opposite their place.

Marmalade and jam

It is great if you can make your own marmalade and jam, but you can also buy good home-made products in the local farmers' market. Try to keep serving this excellent local produce as long as possible, before everyone is forced to eat from sealed packs of tasteless jelly on the grounds that it is 'more hygienic'. It probably is more hygienic, but it is certainly not nearly as delicious.

Honey

Try to source some local honey, to be spread on white or brown toast, made by bread cut from the loaf. Sliced bread makes regular looking pieces of toast, but it tastes boring compared to that made from bread cut from the loaf.

I don't usually bother with serving croissants and rolls. I have produced these in the past for German and Dutch guests, but they always choose to have toast.

GUESTS WHO DON'T EAT BREAKFAST

I am occasionally asked to make a reduction in my price if the guest has no breakfast, or only 'tea and toast'. I am reluctant to do this as the 'tea and toast' is often quite substantial, with a bit of orange juice as well, maybe, and perhaps just a packet of cereal. I do have one or two hard working regular guests who need to leave very early, and are prepared to do so without even coming into the dining room. I am prepared to make a slight reduction in cost to them, but not the other sort.

SERVING EVENING MEALS

I find that the demand for evening meals is falling off rapidly these days. There are so many places where you can find somewhere to eat now. Your guests may ask you for recommendations about where to eat in the area. It is a good idea to tuck some cards from places you have enjoyed into the guest information pack in the bedroom.

It is usually the lone travellers, often women, who want to eat a meal in, or those with very young children. You will have to make up your own mind about this, because if lone travellers can eat in, they may well choose to come to your Bed and Breakfast regularly, knowing that they do not have to face venturing out alone in search of a meal in a strange town.

Reasons why guests might want an evening meal

You often never know why people are staying in a Bed and Breakfast. Possibly they have been recently bereaved, deserted, have just attended a funeral, or are visiting friends or relatives who are very ill. They may be in your area because they have work to do there, perhaps they are clearing out a house, perhaps they are helping out with grandchildren in a crisis, or taking an elderly relative out for the day. All very tiring occupations. If such people turn up and they want a quiet meal in, I am happy to provide it.

Finding out what sort of evening meal is required

When I am taking the booking, I suggest an evening meal on arrival. If this is accepted, which is not very often these days, I then suggest a few dishes I like preparing. More often than not one of these suggestions is taken up, which means you know you will be offering something that the guest is expecting and likes. Generally, guests just expect a nice home-cooked meal to be put in front of them, and they will be delighted if you make suggestions, and this will avoid you providing the one and only dish they really do not like. If you are operating on your own, you will probably not be able to offer too much choice, with a different this and that for each person. Be firm about what you can provide. They can always choose to go off and find a restaurant somewhere.

Making sandwiches

I offer to make sandwiches for young children, with a view to providing a later supper for their parents. This means the parents can relax upstairs with the children until they fall asleep. Then the parents are set for a peaceful meal. Very often all they want is home-made soup, rolls and cheese, with some fruit, and the chance to chat together.

I aim to be family friendly and I am prepared to put myself out to meet their needs, but if you object to preparing a meal late in the evening, don't offer it. It will not be expected, but if you choose to provide it, I can assure you it will be much appreciated.

Serving alcohol

You are not permitted to sell alcohol to guests in your Bed and Breakfast, unless you have obtained a licence to do this. Getting such a licence for a small Bed and Breakfast is entirely unnecessary, and no one would expect you to be licensed. There is, however, nothing to prevent you providing your guests with glasses and a bottle opener so that they can open their own wine. You will be offered a glass, almost certainly, and sharing just the one glass of wine with my guests is enough for me. You are being sociable without getting too pally.

Ideas for the evening meal

I always aim to provide the sort of evening meal that can be dished up at the table by the guests themselves.

You must make sure that the plates are well warmed. If you set out a cold dessert and some cheese and biscuits on the side, or at the end of the table if there is space, you can leave your guests in peace to enjoy their meal. I always provide some interesting bread or rolls and butter. This means you can disappear with a good book or your television as soon as you have served the hot course. But stay within earshot in case you have forgotten something important.

The basic ingredients for an evening meal should not cost you more than half the amount you are charging for it. Of course, if your guest, or better still, guests, eat in for several days, you can balance a cheaper meal one night against the cost of a more lavish one the next day.

I try to encourage guests to choose a menu that I am happy to eat up myself the next day, if there is anything left over. When I was cooking evening meals regularly, I ended up eating a lot of delicious omelettes made by frying up leftover vegetables with eggs. These became quite exotic as I experimented with the addition of coriander and mint. They made a perfect supper for me with a simple salad and bread.

You should always provide glasses and a jug of iced water on the table, even if your guests are providing their own wine to drink. The rolls and bread can be used up for toast in the morning if they are not eaten. Make sure the tomato and brown sauces are nearby.

Laying the table
I provide paper napkins when laying the breakfast table. Always use the three-ply type, one- and two-ply napkins seem rather cheap and flimsy. I put out fabric napkins for evening meals to make it a bit more special. There is a cloth on the table for breakfast, but in the evening I leave the table bare and polished.

Be sure to check any table mats that you are using. They must be absolutely clean, and replaced the moment they show signs of looking tired.

I always try to make the evening meal a little bit special, even if the food is simple. Putting candles and a small vase of flowers on the table make a lot of difference.

Vegetarian/vegan menus

You will need to find out what sort of menu is going to appeal to vegetarians and vegans. It is essential to remember to keep anything that you are cooking for them completely separate from any other food being prepared, if this other food contains any form of animal product. You cannot, for example, fry eggs for a vegetarian in a pan that you have just used for cooking sausages and bacon. You must use a separate pan, and be sure to use separate serving spoons. Vegetarians and vegans will not, for example, help themselves to the vegetables on the table with a spoon that may have come into contact with the roast meat.

Look for some vegan cookery books to study, you will find some interesting recipes. If you don't want to buy these, borrow from your local library. Vegan and vegetarian food is increasing in popularity. It is varied, colourful and usually absolutely delicious, as well as being very good for you.

PACKED LUNCHES

When I first started running a Bed and Breakfast I used to be regularly asked to provide packed lunches. Now this does not happen as food is so readily obtainable almost everywhere. If I was asked, I would provide the following, each portion wrapped individually and put into a plastic bag:

◆ two filled rolls
◆ a slice of home-made cake, or some wrapped chocolate biscuits

◆ a banana or an apple

◆ a bottle of water, or the guest's flask filled with tea or coffee

◆ two or three paper napkins.

FOOD IN THE BEDROOM

Guests will occasionally bring in takeaway food to eat in their bedrooms. I do prefer to be asked about this, but I would not refuse permission, and I usually offer to provide a plate and some paper napkins. They are the ones who have to sleep with the smell in their room. I can easily get rid of food smells the next day.

Guests who have to work late often collect takeaways to eat in front of the television, with a beer. A bit of give and take towards your guests goes a long way. You want their money, they want their takeaway in comfort after a hard day's work.

People travelling with babies often request a bit of space in the fridge for their supplies, so be prepared for this. Make sure they don't leave it behind.

LOCALLY SOURCED PRODUCE

If you advertise that you are providing locally sourced produce, you must be honest and do just this. In any case, locally produced food is likely to be far superior in taste to that from the supermarket and often the same price or cheaper. In the case of vegetables and fruit, it is often cheaper to buy locally. Show off your local produce. Be proud of freshly picked vegetables and locally reared meat.

I once booked into a Bed and Breakfast that promised on its website to offer me a 'basket of assorted home-baked breads' for my breakfast. I was not impressed when these turned out to be no more than triangles of fried sliced bread arranged around my plate of bacon and eggs! This was most disappointing, as well as dishonest. The same place provided just one each of tea bag, sugar and milk on my hospitality tray. No hint of a biscuit. I would not book in there ever again.

If you advertise something in your brochure or on your website, you must be prepared to provide it.

EATING WITH YOUR GUESTS

I seldom accept an invitation to eat with my guests, if they ask me, which they frequently do. For a start, cooking is hard work and you need to concentrate to get it right, not be trying to socialise at the same time.

I believe in keeping everything to do with my guests on a business footing. Anyway, I do not enjoy sharing a meal with strangers.

If the whole idea of providing an evening meal daunts you, or you feel that it would interfere with your family life, forget it. It is an addition to Bed and Breakfast, not an expectation, that will be mainly taken up by families with young children or people travelling on their own. If you enjoy cooking, then offer an evening meal. Good home cooking never fails to please.

I hope this chapter has given you some good pointers towards pleasing your guests with the breakfast you provide for them, and some idea about whether you would like to offer evening meals.

If you are a talented cook, and love it, then you could build up your whole Bed and Breakfast business on the basis of your excellent evening meals, and you will be able to charge accordingly. You might earn quite a nice little reputation offering wonderful dinners, and a charming bedroom to follow, not to mention a delicious breakfast the next morning

Here are some things to consider when providing breakfasts and/ or evening meals.

- Everything you use for cooking and serving must be very clean.

- Provide an interesting assortment of starters before the cooked breakfast, plus freshly squeezed fruit juice.

- Have menu suggestions ready when guests request an evening meal.

- Buy and serve locally sourced, fresh produce whenever this is possible.

- Take care to store food correctly in the fridge.

- Attend your local council's Food Safety and Hygiene course.

- Have a flexible attitude to parents with young children when providing their evening meal.

- Try to organise the meal so your guest can eat undisturbed.

7

Your Personal Safety

I debated whether to put in this chapter. I really do not want to frighten anyone off running a Bed and Breakfast by painting all sorts of unpleasant or dangerous scenarios that will most likely never happen in a lifetime of being a landlady. But I also feel that this book would not be complete unless I touched on some of the possible situations when you may actually find yourself in personal danger. Or, more likely, when you imagine you may be in danger.

I am frequently asked by people who know I run a Bed and Breakfast, whether I feel safe taking strangers into my home. Well, the short answer is: no, I do not always feel completely safe. But I do not think this risk should prevent anyone running a Bed and Breakfast, provided you take sensible precautions. There are many of these that you will learn to take without thinking too much about them. It will soon become second nature to you to become aware.

But if the idea of being alone in a house with strangers scares you, you will not enjoy being a Bed and Breakfast landlady. Consider taking a friend into the business with you, or the possibility of a lodger who you know and trust, who will be sleeping in the house. Failing that, forget the idea altogether.

TAKING PRECAUTIONS

When you take strangers into your home you are always running a slight risk. Of course you are. What do you know about them? What do they know about you, for that matter? There is absolutely no sure way of knowing what people's real intentions are. However, statistics show that the vast majority of people who book into a Bed and Breakfast will be as law abiding and genuine in their intentions as you are yourself.

You will have to learn to trust your own judgement. Running a Bed and Breakfast does enable you to get a feel about people. Always go with what your instinct tells you.

Warnings from the TIC

The staff at your local TIC will usually be good judges of people. They are accustomed to dealing with all sorts. They may occasionally either not send guests to you, or they may even let you know informally about their misgivings: 'Not sure you are going to want this one,' they may say to you on the phone (although not of course if the person concerned is standing in front of them). Be warned, don't ask any more questions. Just say that you are, unfortunately, fully booked.

Phone calls you don't like

You may one day receive a phone call for a booking, or answer the doorbell, and something about the person either on the other end of the phone, or standing on your doorstep will strike you as not quite right. If you were a dog, your hackles would rise. As you are not, you will just feel slightly wary, something will nag at you to be careful. You may not even be able to put a finger on what it is that you are uneasy about. If this happens, play safe and say firmly and politely that you are fully booked. Say goodbye, close the front door, or put the phone down. If the caller goes away you may or may not have been right. If they persist and ring the bell or the phone again, you were probably right to refuse them. Don't be so polite the second time.

I have happily taken in people who have rung at the door on dark, wet evenings, but I have also refused quite a few. Go by your instincts. Do not hesitate in your manner and do not allow anyone to persuade you that you might have a vacancy after all. It is your house, your safety and your choice whether you offer someone a room or not. Of course, there is always the risk that you may accept a perfectly normal phone booking, you think, and then find that you do not like the look of the person who turns up. But you have accepted the booking, so all you can do under these circumstances is to be very much on your guard. Your first impression may well be wrong, but be careful.

Persistent requests

Be wary of anyone who, on being told that you have no vacancies, goes on to ask when you will have a vacancy. This could mean that they genuinely want to come to the area for some reason but can be flexible about the date, but it could also mean that they are homeless. Very remotely, it could also mean that they have some ulterior motive for wanting to book into your accommodation. You don't want them, so be firm. Say you are fully booked for several weeks ahead, and then you will be away on holiday. Then, politely say goodbye and ring off, or close the front door.

Specifying both the date of arrival and the date of departure

It is very important that you not only agree with your guest a date of arrival, but also their date of departure. This is essential unless you are very sure about the person you are dealing with. Sometimes you may be quite happy if a guest is not sure whether he will be leaving you on Tuesday or Wednesday, for example. You will probably be hoping it will be Wednesday. But if you do not know the guest, you should agree the date of departure, preferably in writing, when you make the booking. You may well agree to be flexible about the departure once you have assessed the person, but you may well also be looking forward to their departure, and have no wish to extend their stay. You do not have to extend anyone's stay with you, beyond the time you have agreed to have them. You should just tell them politely that you are very sorry, but the room has been booked by another guest as from their agreed date of departure, and that you don't have any other rooms available either.

If you take someone in without agreeing their date of departure, preferably in writing, then you are running the risk of them not being willing to leave. Quite possibly they cannot find anywhere else to move to, or else they may be unable or unwilling to pay for the room, and they are putting off the day they have to tell you this. Or, they are planning to leave at their own convenience without your knowledge, so they won't have to face the bill at all.

You should ask them how long they wish to stay, take the money from them for this length of time, and give them a receipt for the money received. When this agreed time is up, you should ask them to leave, unless you are willing for them to stay. In this case, agree another few days and take the money up front, again giving a receipt for the money taken and showing the departure date. This way, if things go really wrong, you have your copy of the receipt to prove that they are in breach of the agreement.

This may sound pedantic, but I would be extremely careful about taking anyone into my Bed and Breakfast with an open-ended departure date.

Take notice of any warnings

Recently I received a warning phone call from a neighbouring Bed and Breakfast about a man who was doing the rounds of the local Bed and Breakfasts. The story was that he had been thrown out of his home by his wife. He was trawling all the local Bed and Breakfasts to find a room. When he was asked to pay for the room up front he would say he was going off to the cashpoint to get the money later that afternoon. In fact, his wife had kept his credit card, and he had no access to cash, if indeed there was any cash in the account. He was, in fact, just going around the corner to harangue his wife again on his mobile phone. Poor chap, he really had a domestic situation to sort out. But don't get involved, it is not your problem. I heeded the warning when he turned up a day later on my doorstep, and refused him. I am glad I was warned, he appeared very normal and charming. I could easily have been taken in by him.

Homeless people

People who are homeless, for whatever reason, should be looking for a place that takes in longer term lodgers, or a hostel. There are organisations that will help people who find themselves homeless, for whatever reason. You may, in fact, be approached by such organisations to see if you would be willing to take in people they are trying to help. The organisation may even be offering to pay you on behalf of the person involved. But I do not advise you to accept. You are a Bed and Breakfast. People stay with you for agreed periods, and are people that you have judged to be genuine and to have a good reason for wanting to use your Bed and Breakfast.

Be especially wary of lone women with children asking you for 'just a few days'. It will be very difficult to force them to leave when you eventually realise that they are using you until something better turns up. What are you going to do if nothing better does turn up? These people may well be cunning enough to pay you sufficient money to stay just a bit longer, or they may even offer to pay you in advance. It won't necessarily be a lack of ability to pay you that will make you want them to leave.

I have had personal experience of this problem. The children ran riot through the house, while their mother was constantly asking to borrow the use of my kitchen to prepare food for them, and to do her washing in the sink. Once you have let them take up residence in your Bed and Breakfast, lone women sometimes produce a boyfriend to share the room, so the problem gets worse. You may well feel intimidated and outnumbered, as well as foolish for having let her in in the first place. My whole business was put on hold when I got myself into this situation. I hardly dared leave the house. Thankfully, the woman decided to leave before I became completely desperate, and she did in fact pay me everything I was owed. But it was an unpleasant experience that I would never allow to be repeated. That is one reason why I advise you not to become overflow accommodation for organisations who have to find accommodation for the homeless. Better to be short of guests – and cash for yourself – until a genuine guest turns up.

Non-payers

Other Bed and Breakfast owners will often warn you about non-payers, if they have had experience of them. These people often stay around the same area, going from one Bed and Breakfast to another, and leaving without paying the bill. They appear to be pleasant and plausible, but they are nevertheless crooks, and what they are doing is theft. They are stealing from you. So if you get this sort of information, pass it on to others. If you are unlucky enough to experience non-payers, tell the police.

Some non-payers are so regular that they become well known enough for the local paper to put out a warning to local businesses. Take careful note of the description given by the paper and be wary.

Note vehicle registration numbers

It is a sensible precaution, if possible, to note the registration number of the guest's car or motorcycle. You should also have a note of the guest's address and phone number. I always keep these on file for a few months, in case I need to refer to them – you never know. Leaving a Bed and Breakfast without paying the bill is theft. There is no doubt about this, so report it to the police at once if it happens to you, and make sure you have as much detail about the guest as possible. Yes, I realise it may be false information that you have been given, but at least you will be able to give the police evidence that you have behaved responsibly, and you might just give them the last bit of information they need to make an arrest.

Have a professional attitude

You can increase your own safety by always having a professional attitude to your guests. Do not ever be too familiar or over-friendly. I always politely refuse to become involved in conversations of a personal nature. I side step questions about myself or my family if I do not feel the questions are appropriate.

Remember as you read this, that it is most likely that all the people visiting your Bed and Breakfast will be entirely genuine and many will be very pleasant. Just be cautious.

Do not advertise that you are on your own

If you are running the business on your own there is no need to reveal this fact. Who is to know who else is living in the house with you? You are certainly not going to tell them, even if you are asked outright. I have been known to invent a partner or a husband who is due back home later. He can always be delayed, can't he? Sometimes, I invent a son-in-law who lives in the same road, and mention that he may be calling round. It is often wise to mention that you have family in the same town. No one is to know that this is pure fiction.

Creating an impression of other occupants

It is quite easy to create an impression that you are not living on your own running the business single-handedly and that the house is certainly not empty.

When the guest arrives, I always make sure that there is a radio playing or a television turned on behind a closed door in a room near to the guest's. My own sitting room is right by the front door, so as a matter of habit, I keep the door firmly shut and the television turned up quite loudly when I am expecting an arrival. Who is to know who might be sitting in there?

My grandmother, years ago, always kept a man's jacket and cap hanging up on a peg in the hall by the front door for just this reason. As far as anyone knew the owner of the jacket was somewhere in the house, or could come in at any moment.

Locking your bedroom door

I NEVER go to bed at night without locking my bedroom door when I have guests staying, no matter how relaxed I feel towards them. It is just a sensible precaution that you must get into the habit of taking.

Dressing respectably

I would never dream of appearing other than fully and respectably dressed (except in a real emergency) in front of my guests. To do this, in some cases, would put out completely the wrong message. I have never relaxed this rule even when I have been waiting up into the early hours of the morning for a guest to return. Particularly not then, in fact.

Checking who comes in

One reason for waiting up for the return of your late night celebrating guest is to make sure only the guest with the booking is coming into your house. Wedding guests in particular seem to think that you will not mind the odd extra guest who has been unable, or too lazy, to book anywhere to stay for themselves. Everyone carries a mobile phone these days. You may well feel quite happy when the guest you have already welcomed into your Bed and Breakfast telephones you to see if there is a vacancy for another guest, albeit rather a late one. You may feel quite happy to agree, and the extra cash is always welcome. The chances are the extra guest will be perfectly nice, and will gratefully pay your bill in the morning. But remember the decision is yours, and if you do not want to take the risk, refuse to take the extra booking. Wait up and make sure who comes in. It is your house, you are in charge.

WHEN YOU FEEL THREATENED

It is quite possible to have a nasty experience from another fellow human being anywhere you go. Such events are almost always completely unexpected.

Burglar alarms

I have always had a burglar alarm fitted, but I do not use it when guests are in residence. Because so many people have had copies of my house keys, and those who are that way inclined also know the layout of my house, I think the burglar alarm is essential for times when I am away from home, or am alone, but I would find it very difficult to manage if I had guests in the house. You have to accept that guests have a perfect right to get up in the middle of the night and go out to their car because they have forgotten something from it, or possibly to go out to a 24-hour shop if they feel the need, or even just to go for a walk. This could certainly happen on a beautiful early summer morning. You may well not want to rise so early. This would set off an alarm. That is why I leave it switched off when I have guests.

Personal alarms

You can keep a personal alarm handy, which will give out a loud noise when you activate it. These are small devices that you can either hold in your hand, put in your pocket, or have handy in a drawer. I used to keep one on the table beside my bed when I ran a Bed and Breakfast which was in a house down an isolated lane. I will tell you truthfully that the only time it ever entered my head to use this was nothing to do with the Bed and Breakfast. I always carried it in my pocket when out dog walking, and on this occasion I activated it to stop a dog fight. It was tremendously effective, with all three dogs, including mine, shooting off in different directions. The other two owners were impressed!

Calling the police

The police will not be interested in you unless you are unfortunate enough to have a real 'incident'. You cannot phone them every time you feel a bit nervous about someone who is staying in your house. They will however be happy to come along to advise you on crime prevention in your property. They will tell you that loud noise and bright light are the most effective deterrents. So setting off a personal alarm if you feel yourself threatened will probably do the trick.

'Last-ditch' strategy

Unless you have no imagination at all, you will imagine some bad scenarios happening to you in your Bed and Breakfast. These will be worse when you are tired, or when a guest you may not be completely certain about is due to arrive. Your imagination will more than likely create something far more terrible than is ever likely to happen to you.

I have never yet had to resort to what I call my 'last-ditch' strategy, and I really hope that you never will have to either. If I felt that I could not go to bed without lying rigid with fear, listening to every sound from the guest bedroom, I would sit up all night in a well-lighted room near the front door with my mobile phone and my personal alarm. I would make up for lost sleep the next day when the guest had safely left.

You can always phone a friend to come around if you are ever really worried. I am talking about the very rare occasion when you might suspect something is wrong.

As I wrote earlier, if you are a very nervous person, you are in the wrong job. You cannot get your friends or the police round on every occasion that one of your guests behaves a bit oddly, nor can you spend every night of your busy life sitting awake near an easy exit. This sort of incident is most unlikely ever to take place. Make sure your imagination does not run away with you. Take sensible precautions.

Here are some points to remember for your personal safety:

♦ The vast majority of people who will visit you are law abiding and genuine.

♦ Refuse a booking if you feel at all unsure.

♦ Never accept an open-ended booking; put the date of departure in writing if at all possible.

♦ Keep a copy of all letters and receipts.

♦ Always maintain a professional attitude to guests – avoid conversation on personal matters that may reveal facts about yourself. Invent a partner or a family nearby if appropriate.

♦ When possible, note the registration number of guests' vehicles.

♦ Keep note of guests' details on file for several weeks after they have left.

♦ Use radio or television sound to create a sense of other occupants in the house.

♦ Don't run a Bed and Breakfast on your own if you are scared of the idea of strangers in your house.

8
Managing the Finances

R unning a small Bed and Breakfast is never going to make you a fortune. The one thing you are not charging for is your own time, and you probably give a lot of that to the guests. Most of the people who run a small Bed and Breakfast have some other form of income. Many fit in a job around the Bed and Breakfast, if they can get flexible hours. Or they work at home on something additional to their Bed and Breakfast. Or many have a pension. Or a partner who works outside the Bed and Breakfast business. However you do it, and however you look at it, a small Bed and Breakfast will not make you a large income, although at certain peak times, the money may flow in very nicely. Make the most of these times. Pull out all the stops and work like crazy to get the money in when the guests are plentiful. There will be lean times ahead, so try to build up a bit of money for these.

HAVING ANOTHER JOB

It is difficult to keep regular hours in a job outside your home if you have no partner to help you with the Bed and Breakfast. A job with flexible working hours will make life much easier for you, but these are harder to find. Of course, you can insist that you stick firmly to the times that your guests can arrive and depart, provided that you make this quite clear in your brochure and at the time of booking. But this rigid attitude does not make for a great welcome, and guests may well look elsewhere, and find without any difficulty, somewhere more accommodating to their needs. Guests often want to linger late into the morning, especially after a late night. Others on the other hand will be gone by 7.30 a.m. Many guests want to arrive soon after lunch, and those who are attending a wedding, or a job interview, often plan to arrive even earlier. They need time to change, having unpacked and ironed their smart clothes.

I once had a family of four who assured me that they would arrive well after tea time as they were house hunting, with several properties to view. In fact, they turned up shortly after lunch, on the coldest day of the year, explaining that they had settled on the first property they had visited. With two small children it seemed pointless to go on looking. They were very pleased to get warm again in their room. If I had been out at work, it is possible they might have turned around and found somewhere else. They have stayed with me twice since that first time, and are now settled in the area. They recommend me to all their friends, and I often take their overflow guests. Be prepared – guests do not always stick to their schedule.

Getting help with the Bed and Breakfast

You can rely on a friend, or pay someone to come in and prepare the breakfast for your guests, if you have to be away unexpectedly. You can employ a cleaner to come in to clean the rooms. But you will have to pay the cleaner whether you have had guests using the rooms or not. This is not an economical way to run a small business in the long term.

I had to employ a friend once when I really could not be at home, and I did not want to cancel the booking. She practised cooking breakfast for days before. In the end, all the guest asked for was a cup of coffee. But at least he was looked after properly. Running a successful small Bed and Breakfast is very much a hands-on business. Every guest is going to be different, and each one should be important to you.

DECLARING YOUR INCOME

You will have to declare your Bed and Breakfast earnings for tax purposes. Of course, you only pay tax on the final profit from the business, not the whole amount of money you take in from guests.

Net income

Keep this fact clear in your mind. You only pay tax on profit you make. There are many expenses you can deduct from your gross income. Once these expenses have been deducted from the amount of money you have taken in, it becomes the net income, that is, income which is genuine profit to you.

If you just add up in your head the amount of money you are going to take in, you may think you are going to make a small fortune. But you will be surprised how much money you will have to spend out on food, heating, lighting, advertising, bed linen, towels, equipment replacement, emergency visits to the launderette and many other seemingly small expenses. Don't forget washing powder, dishwasher tablets, cleaning products and toilet paper. These add up quickly. Their cost can all be deducted from your gross profit, to reach the true amount of your net income. Just sit down and cost out, item by item, a full cooked breakfast. Remember, you are going to use decent ingredients. You will be surprised at the cost. Do the same for evening meals, if you provide these. Remember, work on the principle that the ingredients of the meal should amount to half what you are charging for the meal.

Employing an accountant

I would advise you to employ an accountant for the first couple of years that you are in business. There are many who deal with small businesses, their charges are reasonable and they will almost certainly save you money in the long run. KEEP EVERY RECEIPT TO DO WITH YOUR BUSINESS. Keeping your receipts neatly filed in date order and handing them over to the accountant neatly listed in date order will also save you money. An exasperated accountant chasing you for elusive bits of paper will use up more time, and you are paying for that time.

You will need to supply details such as your gas, electricity, phone, water rates, as these and many others that your accountant will advise you about can be allocated on a pro rata basis to your list of expenses for your business.

After a couple of years I am sure you will be able to manage your annual tax return perfectly competently on your own.

Sole trader

If you are going to pay your tax as a sole trader, you must register your Bed and Breakfast business with your local tax office. You telephone them with your national insurance number and your tax reference, and give them the starting date of your business. It is wise to be aware that if you register your business more than three months after you have started trading, you may attract a fine.

Rent a Room Scheme

The other option you could choose if your business is really very small, is the Rent a Room Scheme. This scheme under Her Majesty's Revenue and Customs Rent a Room allows you to receive up to a maximum sum of £4,250 per year, without paying any tax. This scheme can include a small Bed and Breakfast business, as you would fill all the criteria required. But this is the maximum amount you can earn.

There is a downside also. You are not allowed to deduct one penny for expenses incurred. This scheme may in fact suit you well, because you do not have to worry about working out expenses and keeping receipts. The tax free sum you are allowed to earn is probably very close to what your profit will actually turn out to be once you have done all your calculations (and paid your accountant). If you have to pay tax on any other income you receive, this scheme could be useful for you.

Running a small Bed and Breakfast business in your own home is never going to make you a fortune. You might at least keep it all simple.

Keeping up with regulation changes

Before making a decision about this, you should go to your local tax office and find out all the latest regulations and details, and keep yourself up to date with them. The upper limit for the Rent a Room Scheme may increase, in which case you could try to get more business, or of course the scheme could be cancelled. It has been running sometime now so that is not likely.

INSURANCE

You will need to inform your insurance company that your house is being used as a small Bed and Breakfast. Many insurance companies refuse to cover you under these circumstances, but there are some reputable ones who will offer you cover without any fuss at all. My insurance premiums are only very slightly higher than they were for the house and contents when it was a family home.

As you are running a Bed and Breakfast you will need to be covered for public liability. Discuss this with your insurance company, and make sure you have suitable cover for the size of your business.

If you have a mortgage on your house, you should also inform your mortgage company what you are doing. I have never found this to be a problem with the mortgage companies I have dealt with, but I would not embark upon a Bed and Breakfast business without informing them first.

WHAT YOU WILL EARN

The money you earn from your Bed and Breakfast will be unpredictable. You can never be certain of your booking until the guest has actually arrived, departed and paid you. The last foot-and-mouth outbreak in this country caused many Bed and Breakfast businesses in the affected areas to collapse. There was no point coming to an area where access was restricted and every unnecessary car tyre or footprint a possible carrier of the disease. Many businesses went bankrupt through no fault of their own.

It is not impossible that this could happen to you. The severe flooding in many areas in recent years will also have deterred visitors to those areas.

Loss of earnings

You could become ill, or someone who is relying on you to look after them could become ill. This will dry up your earnings from your business.

If you have reached the stage of being a grandparent, be wary. Your Bed and Breakfast may well be seen as an excellent child-friendly holiday destination. My rule here is that my family must make their requirements clear, and well in advance. This way I know where I stand when it comes to accepting bookings from paying customers. Do not let your family take up all the prime booking dates in the calendar. They can always visit during your off season.

Bad cheques

If you have decided not to accept credit cards, you must state this clearly on your brochure and in your letter at the time of accepting the booking. If it is a late booking, mention it on the phone or in the email. I have never had a guest cheque bounce on me, although I suppose this will happen one day. Keep all the details about your guests for a while, just in case.

Cash is always the best form of payment. It will not be too long before cheques become quite rare. Then, it will be time to consider taking credit cards.

Theft

It does not pay to be too trusting. The nicest guests I thought I had ever had were a young couple with a loveable dog. I waved them off in their expensive sports car only to go into their just vacated room to clean, where I discovered that they had taken all the towels and linen with them. At least they had paid me for their stay in cash. I am sure their cheque would have bounced. These experiences (very rare) leave a nasty taste. Get over it, most people are lovely.

Remember, the law is quite clear. To leave a Bed and Breakfast without paying your bill is theft. Always inform the police immediately.

GUEST ITEMS LEFT IN THE ROOM

I have always, so far, been repaid any postage for items that I have been asked to post on after guests have left them behind. If you are in doubt about being repaid, find out the cost of postage, and ask for the payment to be sent to you before you return the items.

People do leave things behind. I opened a drawer once to find the just departed baby's complete wardrobe.

The heaviest item I have ever had to return was a beautiful leather flying jacket. The German owner went to great pains to send me the exact postage in sterling, as I knew he would. Use your judgement as to whether you need the payment for postage up front.

HAVING PLENTY OF CHANGE READY

Always make sure you have plenty of change ready for cash payers. This is very important. You do not want to find yourself short of change when your guests are eager to pay you and get on with their holiday, or get on their way home. It is unprofessional. Keep your stash of notes and coins separate from your regular purse or wallet, so that you are not tempted to raid it.

Remember that if your guests have come via the TIC they will either have paid the TIC their percentage directly (in the case of my local TIC this is 10 per cent of the first night), or you take full payment from the guest, and then you must remember to pay the TIC their cut.

WORKING OUT YOUR COSTINGS

Take the time at regular intervals to work out the cost of the food you provide. Look at how much hot water and heating is being used by guests. Make sure you are charging enough money. It is sensible to keep an eye on the price of other Bed and Breakfasts in your area. If you feel you are offering more than they are, then charge more. Your TIC will give you advice on charging, if you ask them. They will know what is the going rate locally.

Giving a discount

Sometimes when you are on the phone taking a booking, you will realise that it is one you would like to accept, either because the people sound interesting or it is a larger number of people for several days. These larger, longer bookings give you the best profit, and you must do your best to make sure they choose your Bed and Breakfast and not one of your rivals. This is the time to be flexible and think fast. Offering a discount will often seal the deal. I always offer a 10 per cent reduction for a stay of three or more consecutive days. This is stated in my brochure, and after studying the brochure several of my guests have then extended their stay. Discount further if necessary in order to secure the booking. Remember, empty rooms bring you in nothing.

GETTING YOUR BUSINESS RATED

This may be a good point to mention the rating system currently in existence for Bed and Breakfasts. If your business is rated, guests know that they can expect a certain level of service. The goal posts for obtaining a rating for a Bed and Breakfast seem to change every year.

If you have fewer than six guests you do not need to inform anyone at all, get any sort of registered status, or be rated in any way. You may choose to attract guests from your own website, or by local advertising. If you want to use the services of your local TIC they will probably want to visit you. They never use the word 'inspect'. They may merely offer friendly advice about anything that they feel would be better altered or improved. Their visit to you will give them a picture of your Bed and Breakfast, and of you. This is mutually beneficial. It will enable them to match you up with suitable guests. They will make an annual charge for advertising your business, and they will take a percentage fee from each booking you receive from them. These charges will almost always be very reasonable, and as far as my experience goes, well worth doing.

There are national organisations that you can apply to for a rating for your Bed and Breakfast. These will grade your Bed and Breakfast according to the organisation's laid down standards. You can find out about further details of what is required before you make a formal application by talking to them on the phone. They are very approachable. If you are aiming for a high rating, you will find the standards are strict.

Some organisations suggest that you pay them to make a preliminary inspection of your business before the day the actual rating inspection takes place. This will highlight any shortcomings so you have a chance to put things right. This may well mean that you end up with your coveted high rating.

All this of course costs you money. You will have to weigh up how much added income you will gain by having the rating –

which may not turn out to be as high a grade as you would like, or deserve. I am afraid the day is soon coming when all Bed and Breakfasts, however small, will have to be graded before being allowed to carry out business. Until that day arrives, I shall continue to rely on my own website photos to give the guests an idea of what to expect, backed up by my enthusiastic TIC – and my increasing number of repeat bookings.

You should add up the number of guests you will have to attract before you have paid off your existing advertising costs, then consider adding on the cost of getting your business rated. Remember these are not one-off costs, they are all annual. I think you will find getting yourself a rating for a small Bed and Breakfast is not worth the considerable financial cost.

TAKING SINGLE PERSON BOOKINGS

You will sooner or later come across a common landlady's dilemma. You will receive a request for a booking for one person only, and for one night. There is always the possibility that another booking may come in for a larger number of people, or for a longer stay, which that one single booking will compromise. But there is also the possibility that the larger booking may not materialise. You have to decide whether you are going to take the single booking. It may just turn out to be the only booking you get in that period, so a single guest is better than none at all. Remember that a bird in the hand is worth any number singing at you from deep inside the bushes.

Putting a double bed in a single room

If you have the space you should always put a double bed in a single room, rather than a single bed, even if you expect mostly single guests in that room. A couple who are desperate for accommodation will accept a smaller room, and a single guest will be extra comfortable. By a single bed I mean one that measures three feet in width. An acceptable double bed must be a minimum of four feet and six inches wide; it can be wider, but anything narrower is not large enough for two people, and might just as well be considered a single bed.

I took in a delightful cyclist once. He was so grateful to me because he had three times been told by other businesses to 'come back later and we will take you if we have no other bookings'. What a nasty thing to say to a possible guest.

Many people travel alone these days, I think it is much nicer to welcome them.

REGISTERING FOR VAT

The current threshold for registering for VAT is way higher than any small Bed and Breakfast could dream of achieving. Paying VAT is most unlikely to be one of your problems. This is in fact one of the areas where you have the advantage over larger businesses and hotels. Their need to pay VAT has to be reflected in the price they charge. You do not have this concern.

I have always found HM Revenue and Customs, and my local tax office for that matter, to be most helpful, so I suggest that if you have any queries about registering for VAT, you ask them for advice to set your mind at rest if you feel at all uncertain about this subject.

I hope I have made things clearer about your earnings from a Bed and Breakfast. You should understand that running a Bed and Breakfast is not likely to make a fortune, but all being well, you should be able to make a nice little income once you get going. It is quite hard work. If you let your standards slip, so will your guests, and then your income.

Here are some essential tips to remember that will help you to manage your finances:

- It is useful to have an additional source of income, provided your working hours are flexible.

- Employ a small business accountant, at least initially.

- Keep every receipt that can be connected to your Bed and Breakfast.

- Be aware that your bookings income can fail due to circumstances beyond your control.

- Calculate whether the cost of being rated annually is going to be worthwhile.

- Always keep a store of notes and coins for change available.

9

Final Anecdotes and Miscellaneous Advice

O ver the years I have had an enormous variety of guests staying in the several Bed and Breakfasts that I have set up and run in my own houses, in various parts of the country. These people have formed a continuous colourful kaleidoscope in my life.

One sad and rather desperate couple came to stay, bringing with them their severely disturbed child. This child woke up every night and roamed through the house, while his exhausted parents slept, quite oblivious to his adventures. Luckily, there were no other guests. I had already discovered that the only thing that calmed this little boy down was for him to watch videos of motor racing. I suppose the noise and the movement were slightly hypnotic. Fortunately, we had several of these, which he watched in fascination. I watched with him, less fascinated I must say, but glad to be of help. I often wonder what happened to this little family, because as well as the problem of their son, the mother was slowly losing her sight.

A quiet doctor stayed one weekend. He was immediately interested when he discovered my daughter was about to start the gruelling round of medical school interviews. He spent a lot of his holiday chatting to her, giving valuable and friendly advice and encouragement.

One night a bat flew in through the open window of one of my guest bedrooms. It was a balmy summer's night, and the window was flung invitingly wide. Bats are usually more careful about where they go. The guest burst into my living room, absolutely terrified. A bat fluttering around a room lit by a small lamp throws up grotesque shadows on the wall and ceiling. The guest was calmed with brandy, and luckily I had another room to move her into. By that time the bat had also gone back to sleep, but I located it the next morning. It was folded up like a cigar in the back of the wardrobe, easy to remove to the safety of a tree in the garden. (If you have to deal with bats, don't forget they are a protected species, and must be treated with care and respect.)

A rather strange lady arrived at tea time and checked in for Bed and Breakfast, then went out for a walk before her supper. After promenading around my neighbour's delightful large garden, which admittedly had no boundary fence, she came back into my house and announced that she had visited a 'nice little park but there was nowhere to sit down'. Luckily the neighbours were out.

Always keep an open mind about your guests. Be friendly but not over friendly. Welcome them when they arrive. Many will be tired from a long journey, some will be coming to deal with problems you have no knowledge of, and some may just be lonely.

When I lived in South Devon, my Bed and Breakfast was at the end of a series of high banked, narrow Devon lanes. Guests often arrived fraught with the unexpected effort of the last half-hour of driving. Driving in Devon lanes can be a challenge for city dwellers. These cross and harassed drivers usually calmed down over a cup of tea, especially when I explained a much easier route to the house. However, this was not the case with one highly irate gentleman. He made it clear that he could not possibly stay and risk his precious car in these treacherous lanes any further. He was off, the sooner the better. I agreed to return his deposit, but I took my time over posting this back to him.

Do not hang around chatting to a guest for too long. They value their privacy as much as you value yours.

The days when you have no paying guests in your house will seem like a holiday to you. You can enjoy having the whole house to yourself. You can relax in your dressing gown and take hours over your morning tea and the newspapers. Nobody is going to pop their head around the door to ask if they could have a bit more milk or another pillow.

Don't forget to take a holiday yourself. There will always be a time when you have a lull in the business, however busy and popular you are. You need a break as much as anyone else. Always make certain to mark out clearly in whatever you have chosen as your bookings book, when you are taking your own holiday. Mark out a couple of days either side of your holiday dates, just in case. Keep these dates clear of guests. You will need time to get the house ready to leave, and to prepare your own things for your holiday. Don't forget to leave an appropriate message on your answerphone, and on your website, and to inform your local TIC.

When you feel you have become tired of being pleasant and welcoming to everyone, not to mention hanging around endlessly for them to either arrive, finish their breakfast or leave, give it all up for a while. Tell your local TIC what you are doing, tell potential guests via your answerphone and website, giving a date when you will be re-opening for business (if you intend to do this), and disappear. Go and do something different, or just relax and recharge your batteries. Try out other Bed and Breakfasts, you will always learn something new. Or perhaps you will just feel smug about how wonderful your own business is, and then you will find you can't wait to get back.

You can always open up again when you feel refreshed and ready. Customers looking for a good Bed and Breakfast are going to be around for some time to come yet.

I sincerely hope that you find this book helpful, and that, like me, you will be able to look back on your days as a landlady in a small Bed and Breakfast with great pleasure. You will certainly have some amusing stories to tell. You could even consider writing a book about your experiences.

Good luck.

Index

macerator, 10
maintenance, 20, 21
managing alone, 15
marketing, 29, 30

non payers, 110

packed lunch, 101
parking, 51
payment, 86
personal alarm, 114
privacy, 60
pets, 91

rating, 125
receipts, 57
reciprocal arrangements, 32
records, 80
rent a room scheme, 120

sandwiches, 98
single bookings, 127
smoking, 89
socialising, 23
sole trader, 120

tables, 14
theft, 123
Tourist Information Centre,
    42, 106
towels, 67

VAT, 128
vegetarians, 95, 101
vehicle registration numbers,
    111

warning notices, 51
website, 40